CONTENTS

Page

FOREWORD

I am pleased to write the foreword to this timely, and indeed necessary, examination of Social Policy within the European Community. I regard its publication as opportune given that the Single Market has come into force and there is a consequential necessity to take stock of its social dimension and explore its future development.

The Single Market programme has rightly commanded public attention throughout the Community for nearly a decade and it is understandable if, at times, there was a tendency to concentrate on its economic aspects. But it is clear, as this study demonstrates, that the social dimension was always conceived as an integral part of the process and, indeed, the Social Charter and the Social Action Programme are testimony to that policy goal.

However, I suspect that the social dimension has not yet impacted on the minds of Europe's citizens to the same extent as the economic. This is a cause for concern as a balanced understanding of the overall thrust of Community policies and their role in society is essential. It is for that reason that I have initiated a broad process of consultation on the future of Community Social Policy and have invited contributions from all interested parties, not least individual citizens themselves. A Green Paper will then be published outlining various scenarios for the evolution of Social Policy over the next decade leading eventually to a White Paper and then to a new Social Action Programme. That is why I particularly welcome this study and trust it will stimulate debate not only within Ireland, to which it is primarily addressed, but throughout the Community as a whole.

Future debate must take greater account of the unemployment problem if the Community is to realise the ambitions of its founders and satisfy the needs of its citizens. That is self evident. Indeed the necessity to do so is underscored by the chapters in the study analysing the regrettable phenomenon of social exclusion and those examining its impact on public finances. They indicate that widespread unemployment, especially if it were to persist, could well threaten the principle of social solidarity which has been such a feature of the Community since its inception. It was against such a background that I recently launched an Employment Initiative as part of a concerted Commission response complementing the Growth Initiative adopted by the European Council in Edinburgh (December 1992). I would welcome public response to the initiative so that it may be refined and strengthened in the years ahead.

The Institute of European Affairs, for its part, has already given an indication through its series, *Studies in European Union,* as to the value of informed public debate on the fundamental issues which must be confronted in our common task of creating an ever closer union among the peoples of Europe. This particular study, centered on the policy areas which come under the aegis of the Directorate General for Employment, Industrial Relations and Social Affairs, is particularly welcomed by me as the responsible Commissioner. I warmly commend it to all those interested or engaged in the creation of a Social Europe.

Padraig Flynn,
Member of the European Commission,
Brussels, June 1993.

INTRODUCTION

From the very first months of the establishment of the Institute of European Affairs, it was accepted that its discussions and publications could not be confined to matters economic and political but must also address the social implications for Ireland of its membership of the EC. That the production of this book has taken longer than anticipated is perhaps a measure of the complexity of the topic. Social policy, as the editor Séamus Ó Cinnéide points out, is neither readily understood nor widely discussed in this country unlike the situation in some other member states where it is seen to be of crucial importance. Hence, the authors confined themselves to consideration of a few key areas which are matters of particular concern both in Ireland and in the rest of the Community at present.

The decision to handle the subject this way was not taken arbitrarily. As with other publications in this series, a working group drawn from a wide field of interests and expertise, was brought together and offered most valuable advice as to which aspects of social policy should most appropriately be dealt with in what could be termed an introduction to social policy in the EC. The working group met on two further occasions to consider drafts of the book and gave very welcome feedback.

In his opening chapter, Séamus Ó Cinnéide outlines the development of social policy in the EC since the Treaty of Rome right up to the inclusion of the Social Chapter in the Maastricht Treaty, and raises questions as to whether action at Community level may help us with our serious domestic social problems. Larry Bond deals with what is recognised as the greatest challenge being faced in this and the rest of the EC, namely unemployment and the concomitant increase in poverty and he highlights the awesome task facing Ireland in relation to job creation. In Chapter 6, looking at the possible future effects of the Single European Market and Economic and Monetary Union, he predicts an even greater need for redistributive social policies in the Community. In his four chapters, Gerry Mangan gives a detailed and comprehensive account of the history, growth and present situation with regard to Social Security in Europe. He pays particular attention to the dilemma facing Ireland due to our peculiar demography and considers at some length the possible effects of convergence on social protection systems.

The only section of this book which moves away from the areas of social protection, movement and labour, unemployment and income distribution is Chapter 5 in which Ita Mangan undertook the daunting task of identifying what influence, if any, membership of the EC had on a whole range of different services and social groupings in this country. It was in considering the wealth of issues raised in this chapter that the working group together with the authors came to the clear realisation that this publication could not attempt to do more than provide the reader with some basic introductory material on Social Europe. The need to develop a number of the themes which are touched on here is made explicit in the final chapter where Séamus Ó Cinnéide asks, "Where do we go from here with our Welfare State?"

We would hope that the views expressed in these chapters, views which are, of course, the authors' own, will generate further discussion on the pivotal role which must be accorded to social policy in a Europe facing widespread unemployment and the risk of increasing marginalisation of those outside the labour market. "Economic expansion is not an end in itself. Its firm aim should be to enable disparities in living conditions to be reduced. It must take place with the participation of all the social partners" (Communiqué issued by the Nine after the summit conference in October 1972).

Noreen Kearney,
Chairperson,
Social Europe Working Group.
June 1993.

ACKNOWLEDGEMENTS

The authors of this study owe a considerable debt to the members of the working group established by the Institute of European Affairs, who discussed and debated the many drafts, and to several individuals who provided detailed comments. All comments were much appreciated, though, of course, the responsibility for errors of fact and for views expressed is entirely that of the authors.

Thanks are due to the publications committee of the Institute, chaired by Iain MacAuley, and assisted by Institute staff Odran Reid, Jean Barker and Mary Cahill. Finally, our thanks are also due to designer Victor McBrien and copy editor Dominic O'Toole. All concerned showed great patience in bringing this book to publication with the least possible delay.

1. THE AGREEMENT ON SOCIAL POLICY: A NEW BEGINNING?

Séamus Ó Cinnéide

To begin the discussion, we have to establish what social policy means, firstly, in EC policy discussion generally, secondly by social policy analysts and commentators and thirdly, a more limited focus, as it is dealt with in this volume. We show how social policy, or "the social dimension", has existed in the EC from the beginning, although ideas about social policy have been developed as the Community has expanded and moves have been made towards greater integration. The 'Social Charter' of 1989 and the yet-to-be ratified Treaty on European Union represent significant advances. In the first chapter we also try to establish a basis for Ireland's special interest in EC social policy. We have serious social problems at home. Do we have to deal with them on our own or can we rely to some extent on collective action by the Community?

"A third of a century of Europe and still no social policy worthy of the name!" (Staedelin, 1990). This cry of exasperation or despair by a trade unionist member of the Economic and Social Council encapsulates a contradiction at the heart of the European Community. It is a contradiction between the idealism and rhetoric of many of the founders and promoters of the Community, who have emphasised the social objectives behind the establishment and development of the EC, and the record of Community policy, which has been concerned almost exclusively with economic development.

To many business people, farmers and politicians, the term Common Market says it all: the European Community is about economic causes and effects. It means expanding market opportunities and certain economic policies, incentives and regulations; and as a result it means better business for some and relocation, absorption or no business at all for others. But that was never the whole story. From the outset the objectives of what was then the European Economic Community went "far beyond the mere creation of a free trade area, an area in which there is free movement of persons, goods, services and capital" (Venturini, 1989, p. 13). There was, of course, the ideal of making peace in Europe permanent by transcending the industrial and military rivalry between nations; but there was also a concern with human welfare and, in particular, the improvement of working conditions and of the overall standard of living of workers. In practice, as we shall see, the "social dimension", as the social policy area is called, has always been ancillary to the economic dimension. In addition, the social policy dimension has always been defined in much more limited terms than social policy is generally applied in Ireland or in other European countries, as being concerned only with the welfare and working conditions of workers.

In evaluating the success of the EC to date, we must distinguish between using economic criteria and using social criteria. And if we choose the latter what should those criteria be? This is not the place to undertake an exhaustive definition of social policy, but perhaps it can be agreed that whereas economic policy is concerned with the production of goods and services, and their distribution through market mechanisms, social policy is ultimately concerned with the alleviation of poverty, the amelioration of gross inequalities between people, or the achievement of greater equality in access to resources [National Economic and Social Council(NESC), 1975], and the promotion of social integration (Boulding, 1967).

In the Europe of the twelve, there are still extreme inequalities between regions: in other words, there are extreme inequalities in the standard of living enjoyed by different Europeans (National Economic and Social Council, 1975). Poverty and "social exclusion" are increasing rather than decreasing throughout the EC [Commission of the European Communities (CEC), 1992]. It is small wonder then that even a commentator from within the EC Commission acknowledges that "the lay man, who on the one hand reads the lofty statements of ambition . . . and on the other notes the instrumental and institutional shortcoming which leave harmonisation mainly to market mechanisms . . . could conclude that there is no hope at all for Community social policy". He quickly goes on to assert that "such a judgement would be profoundly mistaken" (Venturini, 1989, p. 13).

It is clear that there are two sides to the case. Those who are pessimistic about the possibility of EC social policy assisting or reinforcing national policies in tackling European social problems can point to the continuing predominance at Community level of economic ideas and economic strategies, which in many cases have adverse social consequences. Even in Ireland, in the debate on the Maastricht Treaty, social policy was hardly mentioned: the big ideas, the contentious issues, were economic prosperity, national sovereignty and political and military neutrality. This is not surprising considering that for most of its existence the European Community has been commonly known as the Common Market, and 1992 has for many years stood for nothing other than a Single Market. The more recent moves towards greater political integration have only drawn attention to the existing, national power bases and to questions of nationalism and democracy.

Those who are optimistic can point to the original hopes and aspirations of European integrationists; they can borrow Chesterton's reflection on the Christian ideal, which, he said, "has not been tried and found wanting; it has been found difficult and left untried"; they can also point to significant progress in specific areas of social policy in the past two decades.

In this volume, we want to explore the contradiction mentioned above and the two sides of the case. We want to clarify what EC social policy means and, in particular, what its implications are for Ireland. Although EC social policy could be taken to encompass a great variety of policies, our focus will be on questions of income, poverty and income distribution or social protection. In this first chapter we will start with Maastricht and the social policy provisions in the treaty, because they do in a sense represent a new beginning for EC social policy. But it is important to see them as a continuation and development of the social dimension which has been there from the beginning of the Community: we will deal with that next. Lastly, to highlight the urgency and importance of EC social policy for Ireland, we will briefly outline the social problems with which we in Ireland have to contend. The question is: in a more integrated Community will we still have to deal with these problems on our own even though they are to some extent the outcome of the structural change that is part and parcel of integration? Or can we foresee an expanding EC role in the area of social policy?

SOCIAL POLICY AT MAASTRICHT

Article 2 of the Treaty on European Union is a revised version of the same article in the Treaty of Rome and sets out the objectives of the Community in the most general terms. As given here the revisions, introduced at Maastricht, are in italics:

> The Community shall have as its task, by establishing a common market *and an economic and monetary union* . . . to promote throughout the Community a harmonious *and balanced* development of economic activities, *sustainable and non-inflationary growth respecting the environment, a high degree of convergence of economic performance, a high level of employment and of social protection, the raising of the standard of living and the quality of life, and economic and social cohesion and solidarity among Member States.*
> (Council of the European Communities, 1992).

It is clear that the new phrases in Article 2 put a special emphasis on the social dimension: balanced development, employment, social protection, quality of life, economic and social cohesion and solidarity. Following this most general statement of principles it is interesting to examine what specific provisions are made to implement them. There are five features of the Treaty which are important in this regard.

1. It places greater emphasis on cohesion, i. e. dealing with inequalities between member states and different regions.

2. It puts additional social policy areas, education and public health in particular, formally on the EC agenda for the first time.

3. It incorporates a significant reference to subsidiarity as a principle which will govern Community action.

4. It redefines the social objectives of the Community, putting a special emphasis on social exclusion.

5. It introduces new procedures for decision-making on social policy.

These last two points are covered not in the body of the treaty but in a separate Agreement between eleven member states, excluding the UK. We will deal with these two points first.

As far as social policy was concerned the most important part of the draft treaty, finalised by the Dutch Presidency, was that part, sometimes called the "social chapter", which dealt with the revision of Articles 117 to 122 of the Treaty of Rome, the articles on "social provisions". The draft envisaged significant improvements both in the possible scope of Community action in the area of social policy, and in decision-making procedures. However, as is well known, the UK did not accept this section or chapter. To save the treaty "the twelve" agreed to remove it from the body of the treaty. They adopted a protocol (*The Protocol on Social Policy)* allowing eleven member states, excluding the UK, to conclude an agreement consisting of the contentious provisions (*The Agreement on Social Policy*). Although the UK is not party to this agreement, the eleven can use the institutions and procedures of the EC to implement it.

The Community's Social Objectives

As we have said, the Agreement on Social Policy makes two kinds of significant changes. Firstly, the constitutional basis of EC action in relation to social policy is to be expanded: social policy comes to have a wider, more familiar meaning. Going beyond the provisions of the existing Treaties, the Agreement sets out the social objectives of Community policy as "the promotion of employment, improved living and working conditions, proper social protection, dialogue between management and labour, the development of human resources with a view to lasting high employment and the combating of exclusion". This opens up the possibility of the Community having the power to deal with a wider range of social concerns than before.

"The promotion of employment" and "the development of human resources with a view to lasting employment" are hugely important from Ireland's point of view since we have a high level of unemployment and the inclusion of these objectives in the Agreement owes something to Irish pressure. The reference to "social protection" is also very important. Social protection, a term not commonly used in Ireland, means the totality of social services, particularly income maintenance (social welfare).

In the past, the EC has sponsored and managed a great variety of programmes and activities for disadvantaged groups such as the poor, the handicapped and migrants, but because of the limits imposed by the existing treaties these have had to be temporary, experimental or designed only for the exchange of information and experiences between member states. In the Agreement, "the combating of social exclusion" has been written into the objectives of the Community and this means that social exclusion and, in particular, exclusion from the labour force, can now be the subject of EC policies on a sustained basis: the EC will be able to deal with poverty issues much more than in the past. This is a policy area in relation to which Ireland played a key role in the early 1970s, when it persuaded the Community to launch the first EC Poverty Programme.

Decisions on Social Policy

The second kind of change introduced in the Agreement on Social Policy relates to procedures for decision-making. The Single European Act (SEA), 1987, introduced the possibility of the Council coming to decisions by a qualified majority, as distinct from unanimously, as part of what was called the "co-operation procedure" whereby the European Parliament was given an enhanced role in relation to Council decisions. This qualified majority procedure has now been developed further in the social policy area. While some decisions on social policy, for example, in relation to social security, procedures for the representation of workers and employers and conditions of employment for third-country nationals, can only be taken by the member states acting unanimously, other decisions, for example in relation to working conditions, equality between men and women, the consultation of workers and programmes dealing with exclusion or poverty, can be taken by qualified majority voting. This may lead to long overdue progress, for example, in relation to worker participation, since in the past some progressive initiatives were blocked by the threatened veto of one or two countries.

Another major initiative on policy-making is that in relation to those issues covered by the Agreement – the two sides of industry, employers and trade unions, will have an enhanced role. This will be the culmination of a long process by which the EC has been developing the "social dialogue" between the two sides of industry at European level and their participation in relevant areas of policy-making. The "social partners" at EC level – UNICE, ETUC and CEEP – will have to be consulted on all initiatives in the social policy field. The social partners can also take the initiative themselves, and arrive at agreements on social policy issues, and any agreement made between them in that way can be ratified by the Community, in effect, turning it into EC law, or it can be adopted for implementation by the social partners at national level. These provisions on the "social dialogue", Article 3 of the Agreement on Social Policy, are almost the same as the provisions adopted by the social partners at the European level themselves in October 1991 and communicated immediately to the Council.(ETUC, UNICE and CEEP, 1991).

The first two areas of progress on social policy mentioned above are included in the body of the treaty. One is *social cohesion*, the other comprises *education* and *public health*.

Social Cohesion

The objective of achieving greater economic and social cohesion has been subscribed to since the Treaty of Rome, and was given new emphasis in the Single European Act of 1987, but until now it has been pursued mainly through the operation of the Structural Funds. For instance, the European Social Fund (ESF) was designed to achieve some redistribution between member states by financing training and retraining for young people coming on the labour market, and for those who are unemployed. The ESF has been very important for Ireland where a great variety of public services, more or less closely related to training, have attracted finance.

However, as we shall see (Chapter 2) progress towards cohesion has been extremely slow. The operation of the Structural Funds would be, and was, reviewed during 1993 with a view to ensuring that they become more effective in achieving economic and social cohesion. Another protocol to the Treaty, the Protocol on Economic and Social Cohesion, which provided for the establishment of a new Cohesion Fund for projects in relation to transport and the environment, will also have a more profound effect on how the Social Fund operates. This protocol declares an intention "to allow a greater margin of flexibility in allocating finance . . . to specific needs not covered under the present Structural Funds regulations". This opened up the possibility of ESF funding for wider social service programmes in certain member states.

Education and Public Health

The EC has developed over the years certain limited functions in relation to education and public health, but these had a narrow legal basis. In the new treaty there is a whole new section on education which puts it more clearly on the EC agenda (Article 126). The formal emphasis is on promoting the European dimension in education at the national level and on facilitating cross-national exchanges among teaching staffs and students, activities which are already well established. But the terms used in the treaty, i. e. "supporting and supplementing" the action of member states in relation to education, could open up wider possibilities. Already in Ireland, NESC has suggested that education generally should be grant- aided from Brussels since we are feeding into a European labour market (NESC, 1989). We are paying for the education of workers whose efforts will contribute to building the economies of other member states. While transfers for education will still not be possible (because EC competence will continue to relate mainly to training), widely defined, a future expansion of competence which would allow for the NESC idea could be envisaged, but will depend on how the discussion on subsidiarity develops.

There are also new provisions on health policy in the treaty (Article 129). Heretofore, the EC remit as far as health is concerned has been limited: there have been EC education campaigns in relation to cancer and AIDS, and there has been cooperation between member states on research. Now, as in the case of education, the Community accepts a certain responsibility in the health field within its constitution. Again, this opens up the possibility of a wider EC health services policy in the future, but as with education, subject to subsidiarity.

Subsidiarity

In the past few years there has been increasing tensions between member states themselves, and between some member states and the EC Commission, on the expanding role of the Community. The Commission has been anxious to allay fears by declaring its adherence to the principle of subsidiarity. According to this principle policy responsibility should be retained at national level, and the Community should only take on functions that cannot effectively, or most efficiently, be discharged at the national level. This principle has now been given legal status by being incorporated into the Treaty on European Union

(Article 3b): "In areas which do not fall within its exclusive competence, the Community shall take action only if and insofar as the objectives of the proposed action cannot be sufficiently achieved by the member states and can therefore, by reason of the scale or effects of the proposed action, be better achieved by the Community". The European Parliament and the Commission has been pushing out the frontiers of the Community's competence in relation to social policy. The progressive aspects of the Treaty of Maastricht from this point of view, dealt with above, must be seen in the light of this subsidiarity issue. It is not entirely clear yet how restrictive 'subsidiarity' will be, but it could greatly affect the developing role of the Community in relation to social policy.

While we have dealt with the main features of the Treaty on European Union which have implications for social policy, the treaty is still the focus of discussion on EC affairs. But we need to see the treaty in a wider context and, in particular, we need to see the provisions relating to social policy as part of a longer narrative. In short, we need to consider how EC social policy has developed until now.

EC SOCIAL POLICY: THE BACKGROUND

As we have noted above, the Maastricht Treaty represents a new beginning, but it is only the latest stage in the development of social policy within the EC. The Treaty of Rome, which was, in effect, the first constitution of the Community, opened with the affirmation by the contracting states that the essential objective of their efforts was "the constant improvement of the living and working conditions of their peoples": this was clearly a social objective. From the point of view of social policy the most important provisions in the treaty dealt with were the mobility of labour, social security for migrant workers, equal pay for men and women and the establishment of the European Social Fund.

It is quite clear that at that early stage these components of the social dimension were all seen as necessary for the achievement of what were essentially economic objectives. One economic objective was facilitating the free movement of workers across national boundaries: this meant there had to be provisions for the transferability of social security entitlements from one country to another. A second was guaranteeing competitiveness, a level playing field for enterprises in the different jurisdictions: hence the provisions on men/women equality to ensure that enterprises in any particular country would not have a competitive edge because they paid women less. A third economic objective was investment in human capital, and the ESF was established to make a contribution in that direction.

From those beginnings, closely related to economic objectives, EC social policy has developed over the intervening thirty five years through a number of stages. The story can be outlined in terms of the principle milestones along the way:

- the reform of the European Social Fund in 1971
- the adoption of a Social Action Programme in 1974 shortly after the accession of Denmark, Ireland and the United Kingdom
- the Single Act of 1987 which, *inter alia*, placed a new emphasis on economic and social cohesion
- the "Social Charter" of 1989, an important policy programme based on the existing treaties
- the Treaty on European Union signed at Maastricht

and, lastly, in the field of social protection,

- the recommendations on social protection adopted in 1992.

Schema 1. 1. presents these milestones as a chronology, indicating the policy areas which were added or developed at each stage. It is worthwhile highlighting one of these milestones in particular, the Social Charter of 1989 (which is not to be confused with the so-called *social chapter* in the draft Treaty on European Union which became the Agreement on Social Policy at Maastricht).

SCHEMA 1.1.
EC SOCIAL POLICY: MAIN DEVELOPMENTS

1957 Treaty of Rome	• labour mobility • social security for migrant workers • equal pay for men and women • the European Social Fund
1971 Reform of ESF	• funding from Community's resources • funding for vocational training • targeting of disadvantaged groups
1974 Social Action Programme	• promotion of employment • living and working conditions • the social dialogue • first Poverty Programme
1987 The Single European Act	• environmental protection • consumer protection • health and safety of workers • economic and social cohesion
1989 Community Charter of Fundamental Social Rights of Workers (the Social Charter - 11 member states) and related Commission Action Programme. These did not comprise a new treaty: they were derived from the provisions of the existing treaties).	Action Programme features 47 initiatives **Main Headings** • employment and remuneration • living and working conditions • social protection • workers' participation • men/women equality • vocational training • health and safety for workers • the elderly/the disabled
1992 Treaty of European Union	All member states • Protocol on Economic and Social Integration • provisions on education and public health • subsidiarity: 11 member states (Agreement on Social Policy) • wider social objectives • qualified majority voting and more active social dialogue
1992 Recommendations on Social Protection (i.e. social welfare), following the Social Charter.	• convergence of social protection systems • "guaranteed resources", i.e. minimum incomes.

The Social Charter was seen as an important adjunct to the Single European Act, an important part of the lead-up to the Single Market. In June 1988, the European Council of Hanover had emphasised "the importance of the social aspects of progress towards the objectives of 1992". The Commission considered that an important contribution could be made in that direction by the adoption of a Community Charter of Basic Social Rights, analogous to the *Social Charter* of the Council of Europe or the Conventions of the International Labour Organisation (ILO). The President of the Commission asked the Economic and Social Committee to make recommendations on what the Charter should cover. The Commission prepared a preliminary draft of the Charter and it was left to the French Presidency to steer it through the Council at the end of 1989. Initially, it was envisaged as a wide-ranging charter, almost a social Bill of Rights for EC member states. However, it was watered down to become a Charter of Basic Rights for *Workers* consisting of a reiteration of principles and ideas in the existing treaties and not even exploiting to the full the potential of those treaties for the social dimension. Despite that, the Charter was unacceptable to the United Kingdom and was adopted only by the other eleven member states.

The Charter was not a new treaty giving the Community new powers: it brought together existing commitments and was based on existing powers. It is organised under twelve headings relating to workers rights as workers (freedom of movement and freedom of collective bargaining; employment and remuneration; consultation), quality of life (living and working conditions, social protection, vocational training and health protection) and categories with special needs (women, young people, the elderly, the disabled). In addition, it was accompanied from the beginning by an Action Programme setting out the precise initiatives proposed by the Commission in implementing the Charter. Since the adoption of the Charter, there has been an annual report on progress on the Action Programme.

Another way of surveying the history of EC social policy, which we will follow here, is to deal with the main ideas which inspired social policy as it developed through its various stages. These ideas, in chronological order, are as follows:

Competitiveness

Free Movement of Workers

Compensation

Economic and Social Cohesion

Social Development and Economic Development

Solidarity and Social Exclusion

The process was a cumulative one: new ideas were added onto, rather than replacing, established ones. While different ideas have been given more emphasis at different times, they all continue to be of some importance. Taken together, they represent the case for a clearly articulated EC social policy alongside the Community's economic policies.

Competitiveness and Free Movement

We have already mentioned the importance of these two concerns in the early years; they continue to be important. For example *Freedom of Movement* is the title of one of the sections of the Social Charter, under which the Commission has taken several initiatives. In relation to competitiveness, the Charter has extensive sections on the improvement of living and working conditions, equal treatment for men and women and the health and safety of workers, all of which have social objectives, but equally are concerned to avoid "social dumping". Social dumping is what is alleged can happen when there are significant variations in social legislation between different countries and as a consequence enterprises in some countries have a competitive advantage. This can lead to contracts for goods and services going to countries with the lower labour costs and to the relocation of employment to these countries. More generally, it could lead to a "downward pressure on the living and working conditions of those countries with relatively good systems of social and occupational welfare towards the lower common denominator" (Keithley, 1991).

Compensation

The European Social Fund, provided for in the Treaty of Rome, was initially a compensatory measure concerned with the retraining of, and income support for, displaced workers from specific types of employment. In other words, it was meant to mitigate, or compensate for, the adverse effects of industrial restructuring. In 1971, the ESF adopted a more general strategy concerned mainly with vocational training. For a long time the ESF has been one of the few explicitly compensatory schemes operating in the Community. However, the idea of compensation has attracted more attention recently. For instance, in Ireland the National Economic and Social Council has proposed that income support for the unemployed should attract Community funds (NESC, 1989). The Council's argument was that the increase in unemployment in Ireland is, partly at least, attributable to the restructuring of agriculture, industry and services that goes with economic integration and therefore should be seen as part of the cost of that process and borne by the Community (see Chapter 9).

Economic and Social Cohesion

The expansion of the original six member states to nine in 1973 drew attention to structural and regional imbalances. With a view to correcting these imbalances, the European Regional Development Fund (ERDF) was established at that time. The reduction of imbalances, or inequalities, and the achievement of greater economic and social cohesion, have been a constant preoccupation since then. In Ireland, we have concluded that the Community's reliance on the Structural Funds as the main means of attaining cohesion has been misplaced (NESC, 1989). Indeed, if we shifted the focus from regional inequalities to social inequalities, the failure of EC policies would be even more evident; in other words, not only has the gap between rich and poor regions proved difficult to narrow but the extent of poverty throughout the regions has remained high.

Social Development with Economic Development

The adoption of the Social Charter was the most significant expression of the inter-relatedness of economic and social development, which had been reiterated in a number of European Councils in the late eighties. To quote the preamble to the Charter:

> Whereas following on from the conclusions of the European Councils of Hanover and Rhodes [1988] the European Council of Madrid (1989) considered that, in the context of the establishment of the single European market, the same importance must be attached to the social aspects as to the economic aspects and whereas, therefore, they must be developed in a balanced manner.

The erosion of the original idealism which inspired the Social Charter and the fact that it was eventually adopted by only eleven member states (the exception being the UK) devalued the exercise a good deal and undermined the notion of the equal importance of social development. However, the Commission, and *some* member states at least, continue to regard the principle as being of fundamental importance.

Solidarity and Social Exclusion

The Social Charter also referred to the importance of "combating *social exclusion* in a spirit of *solidarity*" (emphasis added). Social exclusion has become a very important term in EC policy discussion, and as we have seen, is written into the social objectives stated in the Maastricht Treaty. It is an all-encompassing term, like poverty, but with a different emphasis. It emphasises the dynamics of social change and of policy by which certain groups are excluded. The Council of Ministers of the EC, on 29 September 1989, during the French Presidency, adopted a resolution on "combating social exclusion" (89/C 277/01). This was in the context of developments leading to the completion of the Single Market. The resolution notes that the process of social exclusion, resulting from structural changes in society, is becoming an ever-greater problem in the EC member states. To deal with this problem, economic development policies must be "accompanied by integration policies of a specific, systematic and coherent nature" and measures must be adopted "guaranteeing adequate aid and resources adapted to the situation of each individual".

The potential for Community action in this area is limited by the terms of the treaties, which deal almost exclusively with economic issues, and by the principle of subsidiarity. Implicitly acknowledging these restrictions, the Council could do little more than *request* member states to implement or promote measures to enable everyone to have access to the whole range of social services they provide; in other words, they were to combat social exclusion among their own citizens by improving their own policies. It also called on the Commission "to study, together with the Member States, the measures they are taking to combat social exclusion" and to report back to the Council within three years. It was on the foot of this demand that the Commission established the Observatory[1] on National Policies to Combat Social Exclusion. Throughout the EC, to different extents in the different member states, there is a panoply of social policies which make up different versions of the Welfare State. Despite – or because of? – all this effort and expenditure, serious social problems remain and some social problems are getting worse. Where are the policies going wrong? Why are they not being more effective? These are the key questions being dealt with by the Observatory. (The analysis of Irish conditions which is summarised in the last section of this chapter was, in its original form, a contribution to this work of the Observatory).

In addition to the main ideas dealt with just now which have provided an impetus for the development of EC social policy, there are two other aspects of European integration, two dynamic principles in policy-making, which are important for social policy: these are the *social dialogue* and *EC citizenship*. We will deal with these briefly.

The Social Dialogue This is the term used at the EC level for the formal relations between workers' representatives and employers' representatives, or the social partners as they are called, i. e. between the EC federation of trade unions, ETUC, and the EC employers' organisations, UNICE and CEEP, and between them and the Community. A seminal meeting was held at the Chateau of Val Duchesse in 1985, which gave its name to an agreement for further progress. The social dialogue was relaunched in 1989 and permanent arrangements were made for realising its threefold purpose of consultation, dialogue and negotiation. Through these arrangements the social partners have been able to make an input to EC policy

---

[1]The term 'observatory' which is in common currency within the Commission, means a network of observers, or correspondents, usually one per member state, who report on the situation in their respective countries within an agreed conceptual framework and according to certain procedures. There are a number of other observatories incuding an *Observatory on the Family, a Childcare Network,* and *MISSOC,* a nework of correspondents on social security, to give just three examples.

development, culminating in the agreement of October 1991 which was incorporated in the Treaty on European Union. Until now, the social partners have concentrated on questions relating to education and training and general questions about the restructuring of the European labour market following the Single Act. However, it seems likely that in the future they will focus more on specific social policy issues, such as social protection.

EC Citizenship The Treaty on European Union establishes for the first time citizenship of the Union (Article 8). This is the latest stage in the development of a "people's Europe". The idea of "a people's Europe" was launched at the Fontainebleau Summit in 1984. It was a recognition that if European economic integration were to succeed, it would have to be accompanied by a deeper sense of community among the peoples of the member states; the identity of the European Community had to be defined not just in economic terms but in social and cultural terms as well. The summit established a committee, called the Andonnino Committee, which made recommendations that have provided an agenda for the Community since then (see Moxon-Browne, 1991). It dealt with three areas: the facilitation of mobility between member states; the promotion of the identity of the EC through cultural exchanges and symbols of unity; and the definition of the political and legal rights of EC citizens. It is this last which came to fruition at Maastricht.

Already, however, EC citizenship and EC "rights" have been given expression in a highly visible and practical way by the functioning of the European Court of Justice (ECJ). All EC citizens can have recourse to the Court on any matter covered in the treaties. The British sociologist, T. H. Marshall, in a much-quoted historical analysis (1949) saw the post-war development of the Welfare State as the completion of the process by which citizenship is defined. As he saw it, it was a three-stage process beginning with the recognition by the state of the legal rights of citizens, continuing with the recognition of political rights, and culminating in the recognition of social rights. Perhaps a similar process us under way in the EC.

SOCIAL EXCLUSION IN IRELAND

Having described the social policy features of the Treaty on European

Union, and having set them against the thirty-five year story of the development of EC social policy, we now need to make the connection with Ireland.

Ireland joined the European Community in 1973. In succeeding chapters the impact of EC membership on the country will be assessed. However, at this point we want to establish that the discussion of EC social policy is of crucial importance to us in Ireland today. By any standards, we already have a highly developed Welfare State, and yet we have to deal with very serious social problems, many of which are getting worse. To what extent can we deal with the challenges facing us from our own resources or does membership of the European Community mean that with other member states we should find ways of dealing with common, or interrelated, problems, on a communal basis?

The EC emphasis on the notion of "social exclusion", especially since 1989, provides a useful perspective from which to view our own social problems. It makes us shift our focus from "the poor", whom we are apt to consider as a static group, a small disadvantaged minority, to the processes by which people become poor, the processes by which people are excluded. And it encourages us to take a fresh view of public policies: to what extent do they counter the processes of exclusion or to what extent do they reinforce them? The analysis of social exclusion in Ireland, undertaken as part of the EC Observatory referred to above, looks at four dimensions of social exclusion and four levels of public policy (Ó Cinnéide, 1992). The following summary will serve the purpose of reviewing the challenges Ireland still faces as far as social problems are concerned.

The pre-occupation with social exclusion in France, and later in the EC, began with a concern about the escalation of unemployment, exclusion from *the labour force*. This is one important dimension. The other three are: exclusion from *civil rights;* exclusion from *social citizenship:* and exclusion from *family and community support*. We can consider social exclusion in Ireland under these four headings.

In relation to the *labour force*, there are many forms of exclusion. First of all, participation in the labour force by women is very low, 33% as compared to 71% for men [Central Statistics Office (CSO), 1992a]. Secondly, the overall level of unemployment is extremely high at 18%

(Central Statistics Office, 1992b). The long-term unemployed number 104,000, 42% of all unemployed (Central Statistics Office, 1991). Between 30,000 and 40,000 Irish people now emigrate every year. For some, it is one of the benefits of belonging to a Community of states where there is free mobility; for others it is perhaps the ultimate social exclusion (NESC, 1991). For many of the unemployed, exclusion from the labour force has its roots in the education system: five per cent of school leavers have no qualifications and over half of them are unemployed one year later (Department of Labour, 1991).

Civil rights, the right to vote and the right of access to the courts, are guaranteed by the Constitution. However, even in this area there are wide inequalities. Provisions for legal aid in civil cases are inadequate; more generally, many groups feel powerless within the political system. At the extreme, Travellers, who have no fixed address and cannot register to vote.

Social citizenship is based on adequate standards of income, housing, health and welfare. Many people fall short of such standards. About 39% of the population at any one time are beneficiaries of income maintenance payments (Department of Social Welfare, 1992); most of them are depending on such payments and living below an acceptable level of income. Social welfare is only one part of an extensive range of social services. And yet although 60% of all public expenditure goes on social services – health and personal social services and education as well as social welfare – the bottom 20% of the population ends up with only 5. 8% of the "final income" of the population as a whole, after all taxes and public expenditure are taken into account (Rottman and Reidy, 1988). Housing provides specific instances of social exclusion. There are over 23,000 families on the waiting lists for public housing, and 1,500 homeless persons (Department of the Environment, 1992). Many of those in public housing are, in effect, ghettoised in sprawling suburban working-class estates, separated from the better off, and with poor public amenities.

The need for effective instruments of social citizenship is all the greater because of the adverse effects of demographic and social change. For many people *family and community* integration has broken down and they are excluded because of that. Over one third of the population live in very small villages or in the open countryside, increasingly isolated and outside the range of services others take for granted. About

40% of elderly people live on their own or with their spouse only (Central Statistics Office, 1985) and many of them feel lonely and forgotten. More and more children are cared for in one-parent families. Many people with disabilities face insurmountable barriers in relation to communication and in relation to access to places where they should be able to go. Fifteen thousand mainly elderly people are in long-stay geriatric homes (Department of Health, 1991) and many people with disabilities are also out of sight and out of mind.

The above is merely an outline of the dimensions and the extent of social exclusion in Ireland. Some individuals and groups are excluded in specific ways: some are excluded in many different ways. Unemployment looms as our greatest and most intractable social problem, but the effects of unemployment for the unemployed, and for the whole society, depend on whether the unemployed are excluded in other ways as well or whether the other systems of solidarity and integration – civil rights, social citizenship and the family and community – operate effectively for them. All these systems are affected by public policy, and, in particular, by what we generally think of as government social policy or the Welfare State. Public expenditure on the welfare state has expanded enormously over the past three decades and yet social exclusion persists. For some, this relative failure is a spur to greater efforts: for others, it calls the whole enterprise into question.

The extensiveness of the social problems with which we have to deal means that it is difficult to improve on our existing performance unaided, or perhaps even to maintain our existing standards. We could make greater sacrifices to achieve greater redistribution, but whether that is politically feasible must be in doubt. Given our "commitment to Europe" have we any grounds for expecting relief from the Community? To what extent are our social problems our own responsibility, or to what extent must social problems and political responsibility be seen from a European perspective? These are the questions which we will explore in succeeding chapters, firstly by reviewing our experience in the EC and of the EC, and, going on from that, analysing the present situation and the prospects for the future.

2. IRELAND IN THE EUROPEAN COMMUNITY

Larry Bond

Ireland joined the European Community in 1973. Until then our economic and social problems were our own, although influenced by our peripherality and by the openness of our economy; at any rate responsibility for dealing with them was our own. Joining the Community offered the promise of greater development, a higher standard of living, some alleviation of our most serious problems. Twenty years later the issue of social policy at the national level and at the EC level, must be related to how we have fared in the interim. In particular, has the early promise been fulfilled; have our problems been alleviated? Here we look at a number of aspects of the question: economic growth and job creation; unemployment and poverty. We show how Ireland now compares with other member states.

OVERVIEW

When Ireland first applied for EC membership, the Community was still enjoying the long post-war golden age of high growth and full employment. The ending of protectionism had already led to a revival of the Irish economy. The expectation was that membership of the Common Market would allow us to share more fully in general European prosperity. However, by the time we finally joined in 1973, the Community was entering a period of recession and stagnation that persisted for over a decade.

Growth rates fell and remained low throughout the 1970s and the first half of the 1980s. The Community recorded an average annual growth rate of 2.0 per cent for the period 1974 – 1986 as against an average growth rate of 4.8 per cent over the period 1961 – 73 (Table

1). Employment which had already been growing slowly (0.3 per cent per annum for 1961-73) declined at a rate of 0.1 per cent annually between 1974 and 1982. The following years saw the beginning of a recovery in employment with a growth rate of 0.2 per cent per annum recorded between 1983 and 1986. Unemployment in the Community grew rapidly in the decade or so after Ireland's accession, with the rate of unemployment increasing from 2.6 per cent in 1973 to a peak of 10.8 per cent in 1985.

TABLE 1

GDP Growth, Employment and Unemployment, EC 12 and Ireland

	EC	Ireland				
Period	*Growth in GDP % p.a.*	*Growth in Emp. % p.a.*	*Average Unemp. % Rate*	*Growth in GDP % p.a.*	*Growth in Emp. % p.a.*	*Average Unemp. % Rate*
1961-1973	4.8	0.3	2.2*	4.4	0.1	5.3
1974-1982	1.9	-0.1	5.6	4.3	0.8	9.0
1983-1986	2.3	0.2	10.5	1.6	-1.5	17.1
1987-1990	3.1	1.5	9.4	4.8	0.9	17.3

Source: European Economy No. 46, various tables.
*EC 9 only

In the latter half of the 1980s, the European economy registered a significant turnaround. Growth recovered and edged past the levels of the seventies, averaging 3.1 per cent per annum between 1987 and 1990. This was still well below the rates achieved in the sixties. Most remarkably, employment grew rapidly, at a rate of 1.5 per cent per annum, matching rates of growth achieved in the USA and Japan. Nevertheless, unemployment declined slowly, with unemployment in 1990 still at 8.5 per cent; poorer economic performance since 1990 has set unemployment back on an upward trend.

How has Ireland fared, given the poor Community performance over most of our period of membership? Since joining the EC the Irish economy has grown faster than the Community average. Irish annual growth rates averaged 3.75 per cent over the period 1974-1990 as against 2.3 per cent for the Community (GDP data, see below for discussion). However, our rate of employment growth overall has failed to match that of the Community (0.25 per cent per annum as against 0.35 per cent between 1974 and 1990). Unemployment in Ireland increased faster than in the Community generally. In the latter years of the 1980s the Irish economy also recorded a significant turnaround. Nevertheless, despite the fact that our growth rate was significantly better than average, the rate of employment growth in Ireland (0.9 per cent per annum between 1987 and 1990) was just over half the average rate of increase in the Community.

Prolonged recession and restructuring have profoundly changed the social situation in the Community. This is especially evident in the increased polarisation in the labour market, the growth of unemployment and long-term unemployment, and associated poverty and social exclusion. These factors are considered in more detail below.

Catching Up On Europe?

Ireland remains one of the least-developed countries in the EC. Average Irish living standards (GDP per capita in 1990) are only 69 per cent of the EC average. On this showing, Ireland is third from the bottom in the EC table above Portugal (55 per cent) and Greece (53 per cent). Spain is placed immediately above Ireland at 77 per cent of the EC average. Living standards in every other member state exceed the Community average, ranging from 103 per cent in Belgium to 112 per cent in Germany, with Luxembourg an outlier 124 per cent. (CEC 1990b, p. 229).

There are some striking differences in trends in relative living standards for the four EC member states with the lowest national incomes – Ireland, Spain, Greece and Portugal – over recent decades. While none of these countries were EC members throughout the period considered here, the reference point is the Euro 12 average. Between 1960 and 1975, Spain, Portugal and Greece were catching up fairly rapidly, each managing to narrow the gap with the EC 12 average by around 20 percentage points. Ireland's position hardly changed at all over the same period,(*ibid., p. 128*). Nevertheless, the growth rate achieved over this period in Ireland, at around 4.4 per cent per annum, represented a period of sustained expansion, in the Irish economy.

Between 1973 and 1982, Ireland's relative position improved from 60 per cent to 66 per cent of Community GDP per capita but this trend was not sustained in the early 1980s. Ireland again grew faster than the EC average in the latter half of the 1980s, broadly in line with Spain and Portugal. There was a renewed reduction in real income disparities in the Community over this period. The relative position of Spain, Ireland and Portugal improved with Irish GDP per capita reaching 69% of the EC average in 1990. (CEC, 1991c).

For a number of reasons, these comparisons must be treated fairly cautiously. First, the per capita data must be seen against relative trends in population. Between 1971 and 1990, the Irish population increased by almost 15% while the total population of the EC 12 increased by 7%. While a faster rate of population growth depresses our relative per capita growth performance, it also reflects positive achievements like stemming emigration for at least part of the period.

Second, comparisons of GDP may obscure significant aspects of the Irish experience. While for most European countries, there is little difference between GDP and GNP, this is not the case for Ireland where GNP is significantly lower. Between 1980 and 1986 a gap of around 10 per cent was opened up between the two measures and this has been broadly maintained since. This means that GDP rates overestimate the growth in resources available for domestic consumption and investment. Thus, while Irish GDP per capita increased from 59 per cent to 69 per cent of the EC 12 average between 1973 and 1990, Irish GNP per capita increased from 59 per cent to 62 per cent (Kennedy, 1992, p. 30). The two main factors underlying the divergence of GNP from GDP are foreign debt repayments and profit repatriation by the Irish subsidiaries of multinational corporations. To some extent the effects of these factors are offset by positive transfers to Ireland, largely from the EC. (NESC 1989, Chapter 4).

Third, aggregate growth figures alone, whether of GDP or GNP, are not a sufficient basis for analysing regional disparities in welfare.

Other indicators, for example, of employment, unemployment and income distribution are also relevant. In earlier Commission regional studies a 'synthetic index' bringing together a range of indicators of growth and of the performance of the labour market was developed in order to analyse disparities in the Community. This index included four components weighted as follows: GDP per head – 25 per cent; GDP per person employed – 25 per cent; unemployment adjusted for underemployment – 40 per cent; prospective labour force change – 10 per cent. (Vanhove and Sanders; p. 39). On synthetic index values for level II regions in the Community in 1987, Ireland was by far the most poorly placed country in the Community with a value of 48 where the EC average is 100 (Lythe, 1991). Unfortunately, the latest report on the regions of the Community does not update the synthetic index figures (CEC, 1991f).

Finally, national income data tell us nothing at all about the distribution of income within countries. Ideally, income distribution should be explicitly integrated in any comparison of welfare across counties. The above synthetic index, by including labour market data, probably captures some aspects of this distribution. Other available indicators suggest that Irish incomes have become more unequally distributed since 1973 (see below).

To catch up with Europe, Ireland must consistently achieve growth rates that are significantly above the average EC rate. If catching up can be achieved at all, it is likely to take many years. On one estimate, Irish per capita growth rates would have to exceed average growth in the Community by 1.25 per cent each year for twenty years to achieve a GDP per capita of 90 per cent of the EC average (CEC, 1991f, p. 41).

THE LABOUR MARKET

Employment

The employment rate for the EC as a whole (percentage of persons of working age, 15-64, in employment) fell from around 63 per cent in 1970 to 56 per cent in 1985. Since then it has increased, reaching 60 per cent in 1990 (CEC 1991a, p. 21). This compares with rates of 70 per cent – 75 per cent in the USA, Japan and other countries in Western Europe. The EC is the only OECD area where the employment rate remains lower that it was twenty years ago. This reflects the very slow rates of employment growth achieved in the Community over most of the period. The turnaround since 1985 is a result of a significant improvement in employment creation. Between 1985 and 1990, total employment increased by 1.5 per cent per annum, adding nine million jobs and bringing total employment in the Community to some 133 million. In part, this reflects the achievement of higher rates of output growth. In addition, the relationship between output growth and employment (the 'employment threshold') has shifted strongly (CEC 1991b). Whereas in the 1960s growth of 4.4 per cent was needed to increase employment, in the late 1980s growth of 1.6 per cent was sufficient. Lower employment growth in the 1990s is a direct result of lower output growth. The low 'employment threshold' has remained stable.

A recent study suggests five factors at work on the threshold (CEC 1991b). These are (i) a reduction in working time; (ii) the growth of part-time work; (iii) changes in the structure of output; (iv) labour market policies; (v) changes in the combination of the factors of production. While emphasising the difficulty of isolating the relative important of each factor, the second and third seem of most significance. Between 1983 and 1986, 75 per cent of net employment creation in the Community was accounted for by part-time jobs, while between 1987 and 1989 it was 45 per cent. Most of these jobs were taken up by women who had not been registered as unemployed. Throughout the 1980s the services sector accounted for more than the total net growth in employment. Finally, the drop in productivity cannot all be explained by a sectoral shift to services or the growth in part-time employment and may reflect "a general shift towards more low wage, low investment and low productivity jobs" (CEC 1991a, p.31).

We saw above that employment growth in Ireland, averaged over our period of membership, has been below that of the Community. In fact, employment grew faster than the average in the 1970s largely as a result of a rapid expansion in public employment. But throughout the 1980s we performed much worse than the EC as a whole. In the first half of the decade we recorded the largest decline in net employment in the Community. While employment grew in the second half of the decade, Ireland was the only member state not to make good earlier losses in this period. The contrast with the rest of the Community is most marked in the latter half of the eighties when we achieved much higher rates of GDP growth than the Community as a whole (4.8 per cent per annum as against 3.1 per cent for the period 1987-90) but recorded much lower employment growth (0.9 per cent as against 1.5 per cent).

The shift in the 'employment threshold' discussed above was not matched in Ireland. At 3.2 per cent, the Irish threshold was double that of the Community. It is somewhat paradoxical then to find that Ireland did broadly match the growth of part-time work and the shift to services, i.e. the factors behind the lower threshold in the rest of Europe. We have to look at other factors to explain Ireland's 'exceptionalism'. The most likely explanation lies in the peculiarities of Ireland's industrial structure. *De facto* we have relied on inward investment to promote industrialisation. Such investment has been concentrated in capital intensive industries while the more labour intensive indigenous sectors have remained weak. Thus "The weakness of indigenous industry, combined with a high rate of profit repatriation among foreign based enterprises, has resulted in a diminution of the effectiveness of industrial policy in raising national income and employment" (CEC 1991b, p. 59).

Unemployment

Ireland's entry to the EC coincided with a period of rapid rise in unemployment in the Community as a whole. This rise was unevenly distributed throughout the Community and disparities in unemployment rates have increased. The EC unemployment rate in 1991 was 8.7 per cent (12 million), having peaked at 10.8 per cent in 1985 (CEC 1991b). The current rate is more than three times the rate (2.6 per cent) at the time of Ireland's accession. The direct impact of rapid employment growth on unemployment was limited as many of the jobs were taken up by 'new' entrants to the labour market (see below).

Unemployment in the EC is higher than in Japan, the EFTA bloc and the USA. Unemployment in Ireland is almost twice the EC average. Spain is the only other country with similarly high unemployment. Most other member states have unemployment rates close to the Community average. Somewhat less that the average are Germany, Portugal and Luxembourg (ibid.) .

Groups most at risk of unemployment differ between member

states. The rate of unemployment for women in the Community is almost twice that of men. The UK is the only member state with a lower female rate of unemployment. In Ireland, the female rate is 1.1 times the male rate reflecting low female participation rates overall. The rate of unemployment among young people in the Community is twice that for the labour force as a whole. In Greece and Italy, the youth unemployment rate is three times the national average while in Belgium, Spain , France and Portugal it is twice the national average. Only in Germany is the youth unemployment rate lower than the national rate. In Ireland, the rate of unemployment among young people is 1.3 times the national rate (CEC 1991d). That unemployment among young people in Ireland is not particularly marked may be attributable to a number of factors. It seems likely that older workers were more hit by declining employment in traditional indigenous industries while younger workers probably had a better than average chance of benefiting from employment growth in new sectors. Also the re-emergence of mass emigration in the 1980s was concentrated among younger people.

Long-Term Unemployment

The negative social consequences of unemployment are compounded with increasing duration. Half of all those unemployed in the EC have been out of work for more than one year (CEC 1990b, 1991d). The growth of long-term unemployment displays a 'ratchet effect', rising rapidly in recessionary periods but declining much more slowly in periods of growth. Unemployment increased between the mid-seventies and the mid-eighties. Long-term unemployment grew even faster over the same period, and so grew as a proportion of total unemployment (Sexton 1988). Long-term unemployment in the Community declined along with total unemployment between 1985 and 1990, from 7.5 million to 6 million persons. But this rate of decline only matched the decline in total unemployment so that long-term unemployment remained high as a proportion of the unemployment total. Thus, the legacy of the very rapid growth of unemployment in the Community up to the mid-1980s is the far greater significance of long-term unemployment at any given level of unemployment than was the case in earlier periods.

Also, while long-term unemployment has declined somewhat, the average duration of unemployment among the long-term unemployed has increased. This suggests that the decline is a result of fewer people becoming long-term unemployed (lower inflow) rather than an improvement in the chances of escaping from long-term unemployment for those who already find themselves in this position. This suggests that the exclusion of the long-term unemployed from the labour market is deepening.

The growth of long-term unemployment in Ireland has matched the ratchet pattern. The significance of long-term unemployment as a proportion of total unemployment is at the higher end of the EC range. While on average around 4-5 per cent of the labour force in the EC is long-term unemployed, in Ireland the corresponding figure is 8–10 per cent higher than total unemployment in many countries.

Hidden Unemployment

The Community experienced a period of rapid employment growth in the 1980s. Total employment grew by some 9 million jobs between 1985 and 1990 . However, the direct impact of this growth on unemployment was limited. Seven out of every ten of these new jobs were filled by young people reaching working age or by others entering or re-entering the labour market after a period of 'economic inactivity'. Only 30 per cent (2.6 million) of the additional jobs were filled by unemployed people. Of these, over 2 million were men (CEC 1991a, Chapter 1).

The experience of the late eighties suggests that there is a large hidden labour force in Europe, i.e. persons who will take up jobs should they be available, but who are not counted among the unemployed. As we have seen, the overall employment rate in the Community is low by comparison with other OECD areas. Women's labour force participation is still significantly lower than that of men in most other countries and averages around 41 per cent for the Community as a whole (CEC, 1990a, Chapter 6).

Women in Ireland constitute a huge reserve labour force. In Ireland, the female participation rate is 32 per cent while for males it is 71 per cent (CSOs, 1991). Participation rates among Irish women are lower than in other European countries, even those at similar levels of development. Also the participation rate for women has increased less rapidly than in other European countries and more slowly than in other newly-industrialising countries (Pyle, 1990, Chapter 2). Existing measures miss some forms of participation by Irish women (e.g. in child minding, publicans or farmers wives and so on). Also the disproportionate emigration of 'active' women is a factor. Perhaps the most obvious explanation of the low participation rates of Irish women is our historic opposition as a society to women exercising their right to work. The labour market situation of women in Ireland "cannot be understood without analysing the State and the way in which its employment and family policies reinforced gender inequality in firms and households. Female subordination and unresponsive measures of labour force activity continued because of this reinforcement despite the corrosive power of both export-led development and the shift of employment from agriculture to industry and services" (Pyle 1990, p. 6).

The labour force situation in this country is further complicated by the volatility of migration. Ireland's emigration experience is unique and cannot be equated with 'normal' patterns of migration or labour mobility in the Community. Massive emigration in the 1980s held down our domestic unemployment rate. The decline of emigration opportunities in recent years has further highlighted the extent of the failure of the Irish economy to generate jobs on the scale required.

Atypical Employment

Unemployment is not the only change of note within the labour market. Employment itself appears to be changing. Considerable attention has been given in recent years to the growth of 'new forms of work' or 'atypical employment' in Europe. A wide variety of changes come under the heading of atypical employment – part-time work, temporary employment, short-term contracts and so on. Though data on many of these areas are limited, there is general agreement that all are on an upward trend.

The growth of part-time employment is one indicator of changes taking place. In 1989, one in seven of the EC labour force were working part-time. The male/female divide is particularly marked with just 4.1 (2.8 in 1983) per cent of male workers in part-time employment as against 30.2 (27.6 in 1983) per cent of females (CEC 1991b). There is considerable variation between member states. Atypical work is not so evident in Ireland as in some other countries, though it does appear to be growing. In 1975, there were some 42,000 regular part-time workers in Ireland. In 1990, there were 72,000 regular part-time workers (7 per cent of the workforce) were working part-time (CSO, 1991, p. 13). Also, other forms of non-standard work contracts are increasing.

The reasons for the growth of 'atypical employment' are not altogether clear,. and probably vary greatly given the heterogeneous nature of the phenomenon. Such reasons probably include state policies of deregulation of the labour market and weakening trade unions; employers' attempts to hold down labour costs, particularly in a recessionary period; workers' willingness to accept poorer terms and conditions given the depressed overall situation in the labour market; the preference of some workers for non-standard patterns of employment that can be combined with other commitments, e.g. childcare; and/or more general structural changes in the economy such as the growth of sectors where part-time, casual or other 'atypical' forms of work have been standard. Whatever the reasons for the growth of new employment patterns, it raises new challenges to labour law and social security that are at the centre of the debate on a European social dimension.

POVERTY

The European Community

Latest estimates suggest that some 44 to 50 million people in the Community are living in poverty (CEC 1991e). The Council of Ministers of the European Community (EC) in their decision to establish the Second European Poverty Programme, defined the poor as "those persons, families and groups of persons, whose resources (material, cultural and social) are so limited as to exclude them from the minimum acceptable way of life in the Member State in which they live". This is a relative definition of poverty which has gained widespread acceptance. It suggests that poverty has to be seen in the context of the standards prevailing in a given society. Poverty is then measured using a national standard or poverty line set at some percentage of average income or expenditure adjusted for family/household size.

Using a poverty line set at 50 per cent of equivalent income, the aggregate rate of poverty in the Community increased from 12.8 per cent (38.5 million persons) in 1975 to 13.9 per cent (44 million persons) in 1985 (O'Higgins and Jenkins, 1990). No later comparative data are available. This statistical gap is itself a reminder of the relative lack of attention the social dimension has received to date in the development of the Community.

In 1985, poverty was greatest in Greece and Portugal at around

TABLE 2

Poverty in the European Community

Poverty Rates and Numbers (x1000) 1975, 1980 and 1985

	1975		1980		1985	
	%	Nos.	%	Nos.	%	Nos.
Belgium	7.9	773	7.6*	749*	7.2	
Denmark	12.4	615	13.0*	665	14.7*	750*
France	19.1	10,174	17.7	9,303	17.5*	9,038*
Germany	8.8	5,238	6.7	4,001	8.5*	5,027*
Greece	26.6	2,290	24.2	2,245	24.0*	2,280*
Ireland	16.4	487	16.9	558	22.0	770
Italy	10.6	5,861	9.4	5,484	11.7	6,678
Luxembourg	7.9*	328	7.9*	32*	7.9	32
Netherlands	6.6	988	7.0	981	7.4	1,058
Portugal	23.4	1,783	27.8	2,721	28.0*	2,852*
Spain	20.0	6,795	20.5	7,721	20.0*	7,701*
UK	6.7	3,625	9.2	5,032	12.0	6,636
EC12	12.8	38,580	12.6	39,492	13.9	443,865

*Indicates that the poverty rates are estimated by the assumptions set out in the source.
Poverty is defined as less than 50 per cent of average equivalent
income in the respective countries.
Source: O'Higgins and Jenkins, 1990.

one quarter of the population, followed by Ireland and Spain with around one fifth. These were followed by France (one sixth) and Denmark (one seventh). Other member states had rates of poverty below the EC 12 average. Just below the average were the UK and Italy, while Belgium, Germany, the Netherlands and Luxembourg had rates of poverty considerably below the average for the Community (*ibid.*).

Inter-country comparisons of poverty, using national relative poverty measures, pose distinct problems since by definition the reference societies are different. One alternative is to adopt a Community standard i.e. adopting a poverty line calculated with reference to average income or expenditure in the Community as a whole. Taking 50 per cent of average Community income as the cut off point, the overall rate of poverty in the Community would increase to 17.4 per cent and all the less-developed countries including Ireland would have higher rates of poverty (Atkinson, 1991). A rather different approach is to try to define an absolute poverty standard for the Community.

At least one recent study has adopted this approach (Teekens and Zaidi, 1991). A food-based 'absolute' poverty standard for the EC was calculated and applied to 1980 data. This approach produced similar measurements of the overall level of poverty in the Community as the O'Higgins and Jenkins study. However, the distribution of poverty within the Community looks very different when this approach is used with the more-developed countries having much lower poverty rates and the less-developed countries generally having much higher rates though the findings for Ireland were similar in both studies.

Poverty in Ireland

Poverty in Ireland is considerably higher than in the EC as a whole. Poverty has recently been the subject of an extensive programme of research (Callan *et al,* 1989). Drawing on a nationally representative survey carried out in 1987 the number of persons with incomes below a range of poverty lines, set respectively at 40%, 50% and 60% of average disposable income, adjusted for family size. As noted above, the 50% measure is the standard line used in EC research and for simplicity that line is used here. However, it is important to note that the income represented by the 60% poverty line is below the "minimally adequate income" recommended by the Commission on Social Welfare. Applying the 50% line to income data for 1987 (ESRI Survey), 1980 (Household Budget Survey) and 1973 (Household Budget Survey), Callan *et al* showed that the proportion of the population living in poverty increased from 17.8% in 1973 to 22.9% in 1987. In fact, all the poverty lines used showed poverty increasing over the period. All available evidence on trends in poverty show that it has increased since 1973 largely as a result of the growth of unemployment.

However, the dramatic rate of the increase of the numbers living in poverty is somewhat hidden by presenting the figures in this way. This is because, as we saw earlier, the Irish population increased significantly over this period. The increase in the percentage of the population living in poverty, taken together with the increase in the total population, means that the actual numbers living in poverty increased very rapidly – by 53% between 1973 and 1987.

TABLE 3

The Growth of Poverty in Ireland

	Population* 000s	% in Poverty	Population in Poverty 000s
1973	2,978	17.8	530
1980	3,368	19.2	647
1987	3,541	22.9	811
Increase 1973-87	+563 (+19%)	+5.1%	+281 (+53%)
Increase 1980-87	+173 (+5%)	+3.7%	+164 (+25%)

*Census figures from 1971, 1979 and 1986 respectively.

The population living in poverty has changed significantly since the early 1970s. Elderly people now make up a smaller proportion of the poor population while there has been an increase in the significance of unemployment. What this has meant is that much more families with children are living in poverty. Irish households with children now have a 2 to 3 times greater chance of being in poverty than those without and the likelihood that children are living in poverty has dramatically increased. In 1973, 16 per cent of all children under the age of 14 lived in poor households. In 1987, this had increased to 26 per cent of all children as a direct result of increased unemployment.

Concluding Comments

Prolonged recession and restructuring since the 1970s have profoundly changed the social situation in the Community. This is especially evident in the increased polarisation in the labour market, the growth of unemployment and associated poverty and social exclusion. The Community is characterised by notably high levels of unemployment much of it long term or very long term. Unemployment fell in the latter half of the 1980s, but this trend has been reversed at least temporarily by the current recession. Poverty in the Community increased in the 1980s. to an estimated 44 to 50 million people.

Ireland remains one of the least-developed countries in the EC. Average Irish living standards are only two-thirds of the EC average. To catch up with Europe, Ireland must consistently achieve growth rates that are significantly above the average EC rate. Irish per capita growth rates would have to exceed average growth in the Community by 1.25 per cent each year for twenty years to achieve a GDP per capita of 90 per cent of the EC average. Unemployment in Ireland increased faster than in the Community and is now among the highest of all member states. The significance of long-term unemployment as a proportion of total unemployment is at the higher end of the EC range. While on average around 4-5 per cent of the labour force in the EC is long-term unemployed, in Ireland the corresponding figure is 8–10 per cent. It is not surprising then to find that the level of poverty in Ireland at 23 per cent is much higher than the Community average of 13 per cent.

Given the significance of unemployment our job creation record is of primary importance. Here, too, the contrast with the Community is marked. Even in the latter half of the eighties when we achieved much higher rates of GDP growth than the Community as a whole (4.8 per cent per annum as against 3.1 per cent for the period 1987-90), we recorded much lower employment growth (0.9 per cent as against 1.5 per cent).

3. SOCIAL PROTECTION: COMMON PROBLEMS

Gerry Mangan

In this volume, we do not attempt to deal with the whole of social policy, we concentrate on questions of income and income support. We use the term "social protection", as commonly used in the EC, to cover what we call social welfare as well as occupational benefits and health service entitlements. The Irish social protection system has a lot in common with the systems in other EC countries, which represent a 'European Social Model'. In this chapter, we deal first of all with how this model has developed.

The second part deals with the common problems which systems of social protection have to cope with as a result of social, demographic and economic changes which have been occurring in recent decades, and the doubts being expressed in relation to the capacity of the systems, as currently organised, to cope with these changes. The chapter concludes with a brief reference to the impact of greater EC integration which could result in expenditure on systems of social protection being curtailed in the interests of maintaining economic competitiveness within the Single Market.

THE DEVELOPMENT OF SOCIAL PROTECTION

In traditional mainly rural societies, the old, the sick and the widowed were looked after and supported mainly by the family and the local community. Industrialisation and urbanisation disrupted this whole support system. Systems of social protection based on occupational and national solidarity were developed and promoted by the state, to take the place of the more informal systems that had sufficed during the earlier era. These systems involve, in effect, deduction of a part of the income of those in employment or self-employment by means of social insurance contributions and taxation in order to provide an income to persons during periods when they are unable to earn an income in their own right. These deductions finance, in addition, health services and family benefits.

Two predominant models of social protection emerged. The model which has been largely adopted in Ireland is that identified with the Beveridge Report entitled "Social Insurance and Allied Services" published in 1942 in the United Kingdom, which has had a wide influence internationally. Before then, social protection had been mainly provided by systems of public assistance under which entitlement to benefits and the amount payable were conditional on satisfying a means test. These were largely replaced, in the case of workers and their dependants, by social insurance schemes under which those covered, in return for the payment of contributions, obtain an entitlement in their own right to a basic income without a means test, in the event of old age, incapacity for work, unemployment and, for their surviving dependants, in the event of death. In addition, all the population have access to essential health services free of charge. The needs of families with children are met by universal child benefit.

The system is financed by a combination of social insurance contributions and taxation. The means test is retained for entitlement to cash benefits only in the case of those who have paid insufficient contributions. Those on higher incomes can supplement their basic social security cover by means of occupational schemes for pensions and sick pay and by voluntary health care insurance. In addition to Ireland and the United Kingdom, this model, in broad terms, has been adopted by the Netherlands and the Scandinavian countries.

The other model is generally associated with Bismarck, the Chancellor of Germany in the last quarter of the 19th century. This model is largely derived from private insurance under which people purchase insurance cover on a voluntary basis to provide them with an income when the various contingencies – old age, incapacity for work, unemployment, death of main breadwinner – arise. Bismarck eliminated the voluntary aspect by making what came to be known as social insurance compulsory. Under this system, social protection is provided for categories of workers who pay income-related contributions and in return obtain payments related to their income when they are unable to work for whatever reason, as well as cover for health services. This is the predominant model on the continent of Europe.

In the post-war era up to the late 1970s, the context for the development of systems of social protection was positive. The aims of social protection:

- collectivisation of risks
- access for all citizens to essential services
- redistribution of income.

were generally accepted. Systems of social protection also had clear economic advantages as they supported economic activity, not least in terms of a healthy, trained workforce, while the redistribution of income supported consumption. As a result, there was a positive link between a high level of social protection and economic growth. Virtually full employment and sustained growth meant that the financing of improved levels of social protection could be maintained without serious difficulties.

The demographic context was also positive in that there was a good balance between those in the active age groups, 15 to 65, and those in the dependent age groups 0-15 and 65+. Finally, given the high level of employment, the systems were for the most part financed by contributions under systems of social insurance.

This positive context for the development of systems of social protection has resulted in a situation where countries in the European Community devote a significant proportion of their GDP to the financing of such systems as the table below shows for 1989.

The disparities between member states in this regard are closely related to levels of economic development with Greece, Ireland, Portugal and Spain devoting lower shares to social protection, compared with the more economically-developed states (Chassard & Quintin, 1992).

It is also instructive in this regard to compare the situation in the European Community and in countries with comparable levels of economic development. In 1983, the percentage of GDP devoted to

TABLE 4

Percentage of Gross Domestic Product Allocated to Social Protection* – 1989

	%
Belgium	26.7
Denmark	29.6
Germany	27.3
Greece	16.5
Spain	17.3
France	28.0
Ireland	20.6
Italy	23.2
Luxembourg	25.6
Netherlands	30.2
Portugal	18.1
United Kingdom	22.1

*State financed social security cash benefits/pensions, family benefits and health services only.
Source: Eurostat, SESPROS Statistics, 1991.

social protection was 13.8% in the USA and 12.0% in Japan. EC rates for that year fell mainly between 20% and 30% (ILO). This clearly shows that the level of commitment to social protection in all of the member states, in what has become known as the 'European Social Model', is significantly higher than in other regions which have achieved comparable levels of economic development.

THE CHANGING CONTEXT OF SOCIAL PROTECTION

The positive context in which systems of social protection have evolved, referred to above, has undergone significant changes and the problems these changes are giving rise to have emerged very clearly over the last decade. All member states face the same problems to a greater or lesser degree in adapting their social protection systems to cope with the changes, a brief outline of which follows.

Social Change

Systems of social protection provide income support and access to services to individuals in a household context. For the greater part of this century the predominant household pattern was as follows. On getting married, the wife would normally give up paid employment to devote her life to care for the home and family on a full-time basis. The couple would have three or more children and remain together until death parted them. In the majority of cases, the husband would be in regular employment for most of his career and then retire with a pension. The wife having cared for the children until they were old enough to leave home could then have the task of caring for aged parents or other relatives. By the time they would have passed on she could then have to care for her husband in his declining years whom normally she would survive. All this time she would be dependent on income support from her husband and then receive a widow's pension on his death.

There have been significant changes in this pattern in all member states of the EC in recent decades. It is now normal for a woman on getting married to remain in full-time employment or to return to such employment after a brief period devoted to full-time care of children. To enable the couple to combine full-time employment and care of children, the number of children per family is now normally two or less. A third or more children can require one spouse, normally the mother, to give up full-time employment for a period, with all the consequences this can have for her future career. It may also be necessary to obtain bigger accommodation, which can give rise to a significant reduction in disposable income. Accordingly, the average number of children borne by women in the EC countries is now around 1.6, compared with 3.27 for the world as a whole (Golini *et al*). An average of at least 2.1 is required to maintain existing population levels. The average number of children borne by women in Ireland has declined from 4.03 in 1965 to 2.16 in 1990 (Courtney).

Marriages are also increasingly unstable and the couple will separate in a significant proportion of cases leaving one parent, again usually the mother, to care for the children on her own unless or until she enters a second union. For example, in 1987, 49% of marriages in Denmark had ended in divorce, 40% in the United Kingdom, 30% in West Germany, 31% in France and 28% in the Netherlands (Council of Europe). In Ireland, the number of women receiving social protection payments as deserted wives has risen from 6,187 in 1981 to 16,314 in 1990 (Department of Social Welfare – 1990).

There has also been a major increase in the number of children born to unmarried parents. In 1960, some 4.5% of births in the EC occurred outside marriage. This increased to 7.9% in 1980 and to 17.1% by 1989 (Golini *et al*). In Ireland in 1990, 14.5% of births were outside marriage (CSO) and in the same year some 18,761 unmarried parents were receiving the Lone Parents Allowance (Department of Social Welfare).

Demographic Change

The major fall in the birth rate now taking place in all member states is resulting in the proportion of persons in the population who are elderly increasing steadily, as the numbers in the younger age groups decline. In addition, due to medical advances life expectancy is increasing and for

TABLE 5

Percentage of Population aged 65 and over* – 1980-2050

	1980	1990	2000	2010	2020	2030	2040	2050
Belgium	14.4	14.2	14.7	15.9	17.0	20.8	21.9	20.8
Denmark	14.4	15.3	14.9	16.7	20.1	22.6	24.0	23.2
Germany (West)	15.5	15.5	17.1	20.4	21.7	25.8	27.6	24.5
Greece	13.1	12.3	15.0	16.8	17.8	19.5	21.0	21.1
Spain	10.9	12.7	14.4	15.5	17.0	19.6	22.7	22.9
France	14.0	13.8	15.3	16.3	19.5	21.8	22.7	22.3
Ireland	10.7	11.3	11.1	11.1	12.6	14.7	16.9	18.9
Italy	13.5	13.8	15.3	17.3	19.4	21.9	24.2	22.6
Luxembourg	13.5	14.6	16.7	18.1	20.2	22.4	22.0	20.3
Netherlands	11.5	12.7	13.5	15.1	18.9	23.0	24.8	22.6
Portugal	10.2	11.8	13.5	14.1	15.6	18.2	20.4	20.6
United Kingdom	14.9	15.1	14.5	14.6	16.3	19.2	20.4	18.7

*1980 – Actual proportions, 1990 to 2050 projected proportions.
Source: Ageing Populations: The Social Policy Implications, OECD 1988.

the EC is now on average 72.5 years for men and 78.9 years for women (Courtney). The preceding table shows for EC countries the projected growth in the population aged 65 and over in the period 1980-2050.

The increase in life expectancy is also leading to an ageing of the elderly population. At present, the most rapidly growing segment of that population is the group aged 80 or over.

Implications for Systems of Social Protection

The social and demographic changes taking place are leading to a significant increase in the proportion of the population reliant on systems of social protection. Many lone parent families and separated persons generally require income support and new schemes have to be developed to cater for their needs in this regard as well as for the provision of housing and health services.

The increasing numbers of older people will also give rise to major increases in the cost of pension provision and health and welfare services over the coming decades. In addition, many of the elderly when they reach the stage when they are no longer able to look after themselves fully will have to rely on community services or institutional care, as family members will not be available to the same extent as in the past to provide such care on an unpaid basis.

It is the case, however, that over the longer term increased costs arising from these social and demographic changes may be more than offset by increased wealth generated by economic growth. It is estimated, for example, that if there were to be economic growth at a constant rate of just 2% per annum over the coming decades, GDP would double in 35 years and at 2.5%, it would double in 28 years. If that were to occur it would more than offset the increased costs of an ageing population. However, if it does not occur to the extent required, it would be difficult for systems of social protection, through the provision of pensions and health and welfare services, to maintain the living standards and the quality of life of the growing numbers in the older age groups.

It should be noted that in the case of Ireland, the challenge posed in the short to medium term by recent demographic changes is how to provide for a much higher proportion of younger people in the population, as compared to most other EC countries. It is likely to be a few decades later, than in the case of those countries, before there will be a significant increase in the proportion of elderly people in Ireland's population. Also the actual numbers could differ from those currently projected, depending on the flow of migration to and from Ireland in the meantime.

Economic Change

The most significant impact of recent economic developments has been the growth in the numbers unemployed and in unstable employment. The high level of unemployment has been the result in the first instance of the weak and unstable growth which the European Community has experienced since the mid-1970s. This has been compounded by the fundamental structural changes which have been occurring in the economy. Technological developments have led to a continual improvement in work productivity which has resulted in an increase in the cost of labour relative to the cost of capital. There has also been a displacement of economic activities towards the services sector where in many areas employment is less stable. Social changes have resulted also in a significant rise in the number of women in employment and available for work. As a consequence of these changes, there has been a division of the working population into four distinct groups:

(i) people with a stable and well paid job

(ii) people with unstable employment characterised by low pay and low social security cover

(iii) the unemployed and those effectively excluded from the employ ment market because of incapacity for work

(iv) non-employed members of the population, in particular, those engaged full-time in and care of home and family.

These developments are also being accompanied by the later entry into the workforce on the part of younger people an increasing number of whom do not take up full-time employment until they are 20+ and to an earlier exit from the labour force of older workers, a significant proportion of whom are now retired from full-time employment by age 60.

The economic changes have the effect of significantly increasing the numbers from the age groups – 15 to 65 – who are dependent for income support on systems of social protection and also, as a consequence, are not in a position to contribute to the financing of the system. In addition, more resources have to be devoted to the provision of training to equip or re-equip those who are unemployed with the necessary skills to obtain employment in an increasingly sophisticated and rapidly changing job market.

Effectiveness of Social Protection Systems

The effectiveness of current systems of social protection in relation to the emerging social and economic environment, is also being called into question. On the one hand there are the criticisms made on economic grounds that such systems give rise to excessive labour costs, thus reducing competitiveness and, as a consequence, increasing unemployment. It is also pointed out that despite the increasing proportion of GDP devoted to social protection in all EC member states, a significant part of the population still have an insecure and deprived existence. Thus, in 1988 the President of the EC Commission, Jacques Delors, stated:

> This poverty stemming from the years of economic crisis is like a cancer growing away at our society . . . How is it possible to imagine that we have social protection budgets that represent between 22% and 28% or even 30% of our gross national income and still we have so many poor people? This is because the poverty of today slips through the meshes of the social protection net . . . The fact is that this costly system is not fulfilling its task.

EC INTEGRATION AND SOCIAL PROTECTION

One of the main influences on the future development of systems of social protection will be greater EC integration. The Single Market and economic and monetary union are intended to generate continued economic development for all regions of the Community in the decades ahead. However, there is a major concern that in the interests of achieving such development, expenditure on social protection generally will be curtailed. Such curtailment would be justified in the interest of both maintaining competitiveness within the Single Market and between the European Community and other major trading blocs, in particular, the USA and Japan. This need to maintain competitiveness could also result in the disparities between levels of social protection widening between the developed and the less-developed regions of the Community.

Monetary Union could require member states to progressively reduce public sector debt as a proportion of GDP to 60% before the end of the decade. This would present particular difficulties for countries such as Ireland, where currently the debt / GDP ratio is over 100%.

While the need to maintain economic competitiveness and reduce public sector debt could demand the curtailment of expenditure on social protection, the need to provide for a much higher dependent population is likely to require that much greater resources be devoted to social protection than has been the case hitherto. Similarly, the problems confronting the less-developed member states, such as Ireland, would imply that more resources be distributed to them so as to avoid the disparities with the more-developed member states widening further.

Conclusion

In the light of the above, it is clear that one of the major challenges facing member states is how continued economic development and prosperity can be achieved through the efficient functioning of the Single Market, while at the same time ensuring that social and economic cohesion is maintained and enhanced, both within countries and between all regions of the Community.

The chapters following, outline the development of policy at EC level to date, in relation to social protection and the prospects for its future development in the context of greater EC integration and the common problems in the field of social protection which all member states now face.

4. SOCIAL PROTECTION AND THE SINGLE MARKET

Gerry Mangan

The Treaty of Rome envisaged the possibility that there would be harmonisation of the social protection systems in the member states. However, in the event the Community has not taken the necessary action to bring this about. What it has done is adopt measures for the coordination of social protection systems to facilitate the mobility of workers between countries so that they would not lose out on entitlements accumulated along the way. In this chapter, we present a detailed account of these measures to illustrate the value and feasibility of EC social policy-making, and its limits to date. It is against this background that the possibility of further EC policy developments must be considered.

Individual member states of the European Community for the most part have retained responsibility for the provision of social protection for their citizens. Accordingly, the level and scale of protection provided, its financing, the way entitlements are acquired, benefits paid and services delivered are largely determined and organised at national level. EC competence in this area under the Treaty of Rome and the Single European Act has been mainly confined to the measures necessary to facilitate the functioning of the Common Market. This, for the most part, has involved coordination of social security systems to facilitate the freedom of movement of persons between member states by providing for the protection of rights and entitlements acquired under the various national systems, in the case of insured persons and members of their families who move to other member states to reside, or for a temporary stay, and/or to take up employment or self-employment.

The first part of this chapter contains a brief description of how coordination operates and the obstacles in this regard to freedom of movement which remain mainly in relation to provision of health care, payment of pensions, protection of rights to unemployment benefits and of entitlements under occupational schemes.

One of the fundamental principles to which the Community subscribes is equal treatment for men and women. This has been provided for in the field of social security by means of directives. The difficulties involved in applying EC-wide norms to the different systems of social security in the various member states, illustrated by the application of these Directives, are described in the second part of the chapter.

The chapter concludes with a brief summary of the implications for the Community and its citizens of continuing with differing national systems of social protection.

COORDINATION OF SOCIAL SECURITY SYSTEMS

The main legal basis for the coordination of social security systems is Article 51 of the Treaty of Rome which provides that:

> The Council shall, acting unanimously on a proposal from the Commission, adopt such measures in the field of social security as are necessary to provide freedom of movement for workers; to this end, it shall make arrangements to secure for migrant workers and their dependants:
>
> (a) aggregation, for the purpose of acquiring and retaining the right to benefit and of calculating the amount of benefit, of all periods taken into account under the laws of the several countries;
>
> (b) payment of benefits to persons resident in the territories of member states.

Detailed Regulations (EEC) No. 1408/71 and 574/72 based on Article 51 provide for this coordination. These regulations have direct application in member states which means that it is not necessary to legislate at national level to give effect to their provisions. The 'unanimity rule', which applies in relation to any measure based on

Article 51, ensures that these regulations and any amendment to them cannot be adopted without the consent of all member states, which is important given their direct application. The regulations also cannot directly modify national social security legislation, but only coordinate what already exists.

The restraints imposed by unanimity and the fact that the regulations can only coordinate twelve distinct national social security systems have the effect of slowing up the whole legislative process in this field at EC level and giving rise to detailed and complex legislative provisions.

Application of EC Regulations

The social security institutions in each member state have direct responsibility for implementing the regulations. An Administrative Commission which meets at least five times a year in Brussels and includes representatives from each member state and the EC Commission has responsibility for monitoring the application of the regulations and advising on the measures required at both EC and national level to give effect to their application and on any amendments which may be necessary. Representatives of the social partners from each member state also have a consultative role in this regard, through an Advisory Committee which meets at least once a year.

Many cases involving coordination under Article 51 of the Treaty are referred to the European Court of Justice; there have been up to 250 to date. The Court has consistently upheld the right to freedom of movement by ensuring in its decisions on these cases that Community citizens do not forfeit social security entitlements by virtue of exercising this fundamental right. However, compliance with the Court's Judgements has at times added significantly to the administrative complexity involved in providing for the protection of such entitlements on an agreed basis.

Scope of the Regulations

The regulations apply to EC nationals as well as refugees or stateless persons, who are or have been employed or self-employed and to members of the families of these persons, irrespective of nationality.

The Commission has submitted proposals to the Council to extend the scope of the regulations to cover students and persons who have never been economically active, such as disabled persons (O.J. C46, 20.02.92).

The Regulations apply to statutory social security schemes only. However, social assistance schemes under which there is no legally defined right to benefit are excluded.

The schemes covered are those which provide benefits in the event of sickness, maternity, unemployment, invalidity, accidents at work or occupational diseases, for families and, in the event of death, for surviving dependants. Certain pre-retirement schemes or schemes which provide benefits to persons in the event of marital separation e.g. deserted wife's benefit in Ireland, do not come within the scope of the Regulations.

Employed and self-employed persons are subject to the legislation of one member state only for social security purposes e.g. payment of contributions/award of benefits, and this is normally the state where the person is or was last employed or self-employed. However, persons who are posted by their employer to other member states to work for temporary periods may opt to remain subject to the legislation of the state from which they have been posted.

A person is normally only entitled to claim short-term benefits in the event of sickness, maternity, occupational injuries and diseases and unemployment under the legislation of one member state. Periods of insurance completed in other member states can be taken into account, where necessary, to qualify for these benefits, as if they had been last completed in the state where the claim is made. Family benefits are also payable by the country where the person is insured, irrespective of where in the Community the children reside. In the case of pensioners, they are normally paid by the state where the person had been insured for the longest period.

Periods of insurance completed in the various member states may be combined where necessary for the purposes of awarding pensions. A pension amount is normally payable by each of the member states where the person was insured, which usually would be in proportion to the periods of insurance completed in each state. Thus, if, for example, in a career spanning 40 years a person was insured for a period of 10 years in each of four states, retirement pension payments equivalent to approximately a quarter of the full pension payable by each of those states would be made to the person concerned.

Provision of Benefits

Cash benefits under social security schemes are normally exportable i.e. they are paid irrespective of where in the EC the person resides, except in the case of unemployment benefits as eligibility is usually conditional on being available for work in the country of claim.

Certain schemes that come within the scope of the regulations are financed entirely from general taxation and entitlement is normally subject to being resident in the state and having insufficient income. The old age non-contributory pension scheme in Ireland is one such scheme. Recipients of benefits under these schemes who transfer their residence to another member state are not eligible to retain their right to these benefits, but may be entitled to benefits under corresponding schemes in the country to which they move.

Cash benefits and pensions are generally paid in the currency of the country making the payment.

Health services are provided by the country of residence or stay of the insured person, but the cost may have to be reimbursed by another member state, if the person concerned is insured under that state's legislation. A person on a temporary stay e.g. a holiday, is normally only entitled to obtain urgent treatment for any health problem that may arise.

A person may also obtain authorisation from the authorities of the country where s/he resides to obtain medical treatment in another member state. Such authorisation, however, can be refused where the treatment in question is not among the benefits provided under the legislation of the member state of residence or where s/he can be given the treatment required in that member state within the time normally necessary for obtaining the treatment in such state, taking account of his/her current state of health and the probable course of the disease.

Limits of Coordination

The coordination of social security schemes provided for under Article 51 of the Treaty of Rome and the regulations thereunder has gone a long way towards ensuring that insured persons do not forfeit social security entitlements in respect of themselves and members of their families, if they should choose to exercise their right to move to other member states.

The barriers which remain reflect the fact that social security systems, labour markets and currencies still largely operate on a national as opposed to a Community-wide basis. They also reflect the disparities which exist between levels of social protection provided in the various member states.

Health Care EC-wide access to health care is restricted by the fact that the cost of providing such care in another member state, normally has to be reimbursed by the country where the person is insured. Thus persons resident in one of the less-economically developed states, where the health services are of a lower standard, cannot avail of better services in other states, except authorisation to do so is obtained from the state where they are insured. This authorisation can be difficult to obtain given the costs involved for the state concerned.

Pensions The payment of pensions by each member state where the person has been insured results in payments in the currency of each of those states being received by the pensioner, who incurs ongoing currency conversion costs. The level in real terms of the payments being received can also fluctuate, if the value of the currency changes. Pension levels are related to the economic circumstances of the country making the payment and these may differ from the country where the pensioner resides, resulting in the payments being received not being in line with changes in the cost of living in the country of residence.

Another difficulty is that the pension ages are different in the various member states and range from 55 (for women) in Italy to 67 in Denmark. This means that some parts of an aggregated pension can become payable before others.

Unemployment Benefits The main restrictions under the EC regulations on the provision of benefits apply in the case of unemployment benefits. Periods of insurance completed in another member state cannot be taken into account for the purposes of entitlement to unemployment benefit, unless the claimant was last insured in that state. This restriction is mainly designed to prevent people who are unemployed moving to countries with the highest levels of benefit. However, it also has the effect of depriving people of their entitlement to unemployment benefit who on becoming unemployed move or return to the country with which they have close ties.

The Commission in 1980 made a proposal for a regulation which would have enabled workers, who become unemployed or who had been obliged to give up their job, e.g. for family reasons, to transfer their place of residence to another member state with which they have close ties, without forfeiting their entitlement to unemployment benefits. Provision was also made for the sharing of the costs of such benefits by the member states involved. This aspect of the proposals is particularly important for countries with a high level of emigration such as Ireland which can expect a large influx of returning emigrants during periods of recession in the Community.

Agreement on this proposal has still not been reached. There are also significant restrictions on the retemtion of the right to benefit of unemployed persons who go to other member states to seek work. These are as follows:

(i) the maximum period for retention of entitlement is restricted to three months between two periods of employment

(ii) the provisions in this regard may only be invoked once between two such periods

(iii) the level of benefits payable may be inadequate in the case of unemployed persons seeking work in a member state, where the cost of living is significantly higher than in the country where they were previously employed.

At a time of high long-term unemployment, these restrictions place obstacles in the way of workers from the less-developed member states seeking work in the more developed states and also adds to the inequality of opportunity in relation to obtaining employment, as compared to workers in the more developed states. There are no proposals at Community level at present to address this problem.

Occupational Pension Schemes The EC Regulations on social security do not apply to occupational pension schemes, including special schemes for public sector employees. Many workers depend to a significant degree for their pension cover on such schemes, particularly those in more highly-paid employments. The completion of the Single Market is expected to provide greater opportunities for mobility among more highly-skilled workers such as executives, research workers, teachers etc. and, therefore, provision for the protection of their rights under occupational pension schemes to facilitate such mobility is now a priority.

The most effective way of protecting the occupational pension entitlements of workers who change jobs is either through preserving in the scheme the pension rights acquired by workers who move to other employments, or through portability of pension rights, i.e. enabling workers to transfer the capital value of their pension rights to another pension arrangement – that of their new employer or, perhaps, an individual pension arrangement in the country where they are employed.

The preservation/portability arrangements among the various member states differ greatly. In some countries, there are no legal requirements in this regard. Where countries have such requirements they are subject to a minimum period of membership of the scheme. These minimum periods vary from immediate entitlement on becoming a member of a scheme in France to up to 12 years membership of a scheme in Germany. Significant difficulties are also experienced in transferring the capital values of vested rights to schemes in other member states, particularly in relation to taxation, rates of exchange and the actuarial bases used in calculating the values of such transfer payments.

Many of the restrictions on preservation and portability are designed to enable employers use the occupational schemes to hold on to highly-skilled and experienced workers in whom a great deal may have been invested by the employer to provide them with such skills and experience. Some of the restrictions inhibit the mobility of the workers concerned not just between member states but also within the member state. As these schemes are for the most part voluntary arrangements, total removal of restrictions on portability could result in other means of providing remuneration being adopted by employers to retain skilled workers to the detriment of the further development of occupational schemes.

It is also the case that occupational pension schemes play a much greater role in providing social protection in some member states than in others and this has a significant bearing on the importance of preservation and portability for the countries concerned. In Ireland and the United Kingdom, where a 'Beveridge' type system operates, many employees have to rely entirely on occupational schemes to provide second tier earnings-related pensions and this is reflected in the statutory requirements for preservation and portability e.g. the Pensions Act, 1990 in Ireland. In countries where the 'Bismarckian' approach has been adopted, second tier earnings-related pensions are provided under state social security schemes to which the EC Regulations fully apply. Accordingly, it is more acceptable in these countries that occupational schemes, which have the role mainly of providing supplementary cover for those in the categories with the highest earnings, are used by the employer as an inducement to retain more highly-skilled and experienced workers.

Given the complexity of the problems and the different nature and role of occupational pension schemes in member states, the EC Commission has as a first step issued a Communication on occupational pensions which provides an analysis of the current situation and of possible ways of providing for the protection of the rights of scheme members with a view to facilitating the freedom of movement of workers both within and between member states. A second communication on occupational schemes (other than pensions) is also planned. In addition, a network of experts on the matter has been established to examine and exchange views on the measures in this area being adopted in the various member states and on occupational pension schemes generally and advise the EC Commission accordingly.

The United Kingdom Presidency (1992) introduced proposals for a Council Resolution on the matter which envisaged measures being taken, initially at national level, to ease the restrictions on portability. Such measures could in time create the basis for EC-wide coordination of national rules in this regard. However, they did not succeed in having the proposed resolution adopted by the Council of Ministers.

Consideration is also being given to the introduction of measures in the context of the Single Market, to remove obstacles to the operation of pension funds on an EC-wide basis. This would require EC legislation to permit for the following:

- cross-border investment of the scheme's resources
- cross-border provision of services for pension fund management
- cross-border membership of pension schemes allowing the creation of European pension funds.

The EC Commission has submitted proposals for a Directive providing for the first two objectives, referred to above.

Cross-border membership, however, is unlikely to be provided for in the short to medium term, given the differences that exist between member states in relation to the way schemes are organised, the tax treatment of contributions and returns on investment, and the regulatory systems for the protection of pension rights.

EQUAL TREATMENT FOR MEN AND WOMEN

The difficulties involved in imposing EC-wide norms on the different national systems of social protection has also been illustrated by the impact of the EC Directives on equal treatment for men and women. Article 119 of the Treaty of Rome provides for equal pay for men and women. By 1974 there was concern that the principle of equal treatment was not being fully implemented by all member states in relation to pay and working conditions generally. Accordingly, in a resolution concerning a Social Action Programme adopted that year, it was stipulated that priority should be given to action taken on behalf of women as regards access to employment and vocational training and advancement, and as regards working conditions including pay. A series of binding Directives on equality of treatment were then adopted in the following years, beginning with the Directive on equal pay on 10 February 1975.

Statutory Social Security Schemes

The first Directive on equal treatment in social security matters (Council Directive 79/7/EEC), was adopted in December 1978 and member states were given 6 years to comply with its provisions. Compliance presented particular difficulties for member states which had adopted the Beveridge model of social security, notably, Ireland, the Netherlands and the United Kingdom. This was mainly due to the fact that under these systems the entitlements of married women, in particular, were more restrictive than those of married men. Such systems were based on the traditional pattern of the husband being the main breadwinner and the wife being mainly dependent on him for income support. Accordingly, the husband's entitlements reflected the fact that he would normally have to provide for a dependent wife and children. However, the entitlements of wives were more restricted on the basis that they would invariably be receiving income support from their husband.

Compliance with the principle of equal treatment required, therefore, the introduction of certain fundamental changes to the systems of social security in Ireland, the Netherlands and the United Kingdom. Virtually no changes were required to the systems in other member states where under the Bismarckian model entitlement was based on previous income, unrelated to marital or household status. The areas where such countries would have difficulties, notably in relation to benefits for widowed persons and retirement ages, were excluded from the scope of the 1978 Directive.

The difficulties experienced in complying with the 1978 Directive has resulted in a number of cases concerning implementation of its terms, involving Ireland, the Netherlands and the United Kingdom being brought to the European Court of Justice. Ireland had added problems in this regard as the 6 years from 1978 to 1984, when full compliance was required, was a period of particular economic difficulties and political instability. Such conditions were not conducive to the introduction of changes that involved either significant increases in expenditure or alternatively a reduction in entitlements.

Occupational Social Security Schemes

A second Directive on equal treatment in social security matters was adopted in July 1986 and this applied to occupational schemes (Council

Directive 86/378/EEC). Member states were given 3 years to introduce the necessary legislation to give effect to its terms and schemes were then given until 1 January 1993 to change scheme rules to conform to the principle of equal treatment. Exceptions for benefits for widowed persons and for retirement ages were permitted, similar to those under the 1978 Directive on equal treatment discussed above.

The intention was that a third Directive would be adopted which would require member states to provide for the application of the principle of equal treatment to these remaining areas, under both statutory and occupational schemes. EC Commission proposals for this third Directive were introduced in October 1987 (OJ.C309 19.11.1987), but have still not been adopted.

In the meantime, the EC Court of Justice has ruled in the 'Barber' case (C-262/88) on 17 May 1990 that benefits provided under occupational schemes constitute "pay" within the meaning of Article 119 of the Treaty of Rome. As Article 119 has direct effect in member states, equal treatment in occupational schemes became a legal requirement, at least with effect from the date of the Judgement. The situation now obtains that equal treatment in such areas as survivor's benefits and retirement ages are a legal requirement for occupational schemes, but have not been provided for in many member states under the statutory social security schemes.

It is also not fully clear from the terms of the European Court's Judgement in the 'Barber' case whether the retrospective application of equal treatment i.e. to benefits in respect of service prior to 17 May 1990 (date of the Judgement), is required under EC law. A series of cases have been submitted to the EC Court on the issue. If the EC Court were to rule that it has retrospective effect, the costs of complying with the Court's ruling could be extremely onerous for funded schemes, particularly in the case of schemes which have had differing retirement ages. The schemes most affected are those in the United Kingdom, the Netherlands and Ireland.

Given the implications for schemes of retrospective application of the principle of equal treatment, a protocol has been included in the draft treaty on European Union agreed at Maastricht which provides that equal treatment shall not be required in occupational social security schemes under Article 119, in respect of service prior to 17 May 1990.

EXISTING SYSTEMS IN CONTEXT OF GREATER EC INTEGRATION

The existence of, in effect, twelve different systems of social protection creates significant obstacles to freedom of movement within the EC and to applying EC-wide norms in this area by means of Directives. One major source of the problem stems from the fact that while the systems overall have similar purposes, they are organised differently, with a major source of difference being between the Beveridge and Bismarckian models. These differences result in coordination being complex which can give rise to extra costs for social security administrators and employers and, in the case of those who move between member states, delays in claims being processed and full protection of certain social security entitlements not being provided.

The other major source of the problem is that there are significant variations in the range and value of the social protection provided, which stem mainly from the differing levels of economic development reached by member states. This explains the restrictions, in particular, on the provision of health care and unemployment benefits, which are designed mainly to prevent EC citizens moving to countries with the more developed systems to avail of more generous benefits. The systems are also based on national solidarity with no provision being made to provide benefits, which are financed on an EC-wide basis.

These differences, in turn, make it very difficult to introduce EC-wide norms or standards in the area of social protection, either because of the administrative difficulties involved in applying them to the various systems and/or the fact that the less-economically developed states cannot afford to comply, as they have to provide the necessary financing from national resources.

The common problems facing all member states in the field of social protection will require significant changes to their systems in the coming decades. As the systems adopt to these changes, greater convergence of the systems may be possible.

The Single Market and eventual Economic and Monetary Union (EMU) may lead also to a convergence in the range and level of social protection provided under national systems in the interests of maintaining economic competitiveness. This convergence could result either in a lowering of levels of social protection generally or, if existing levels are maintained and enhanced by the more economically developed states, a widening in the disparities that exist in this regard between those states and the less-developed member states.

The measures being taken at EC level to promote the convergence of national systems of social protection in the context of greater EC integration, are examined in Chapter 7.

5. THE INFLUENCE OF EC MEMBERSHIP ON IRISH SOCIAL POLICY AND SOCIAL SERVICES

Ita Mangan

We have seen how Ireland has fared in the European Community, in terms of economic development, employment and personal incomes (Chapter 2); and how, against a background of a 'European Social Model', the EC has had a limited role in coordinating social protection systems (Chapter 3 and Chapter 4). In its twenty years of EC membership social policy within Ireland has developed considerably. Is there a link between the two? To what extent have EC policies influenced policies in Ireland? A priori, the influence goes beyond the effects of social protection coordination. This chapter attempts a more comprehensive summary while acknowledging the limits on determining what influenced which developments. From this we can derive clues as to how the EC can be an instrument of social progress in Ireland.

The development of EC social policy is described in Chapter 1. As we have seen the term "social policy" is not used in the same sense in which it is understood at national level: it is perhaps more accurately described as the social aspect or social dimension of the EC. This is not to suggest that it is unimportant or lacking in influence but simply to allow it to be assessed in its proper context. It also has to be remembered that economic policies and their intended or unintended consequences have important social effects and indeed it is difficult to find a dividing line between economic policies and social policies. Some of the social policy measures assessed here were introduced for economic or competition reasons but that does not take away from their social importance. It is arguable that some EC economic policies – in particular the Common Agricultural Policy (CAP) – have had more profound social effects than any of the social policies *per se* but these effects are not considered in this paper.

EC social policy measures (other than measures on social security for migrant workers) were never meant to replace national social policies but rather to supplement them. Primary responsibility for social policy lies with the member states. The absence of a clear-cut, co-ordinated Irish social policy makes it difficult to assess the impact of the EC in the social policy area.

The NESC report outlines the difficulties involved in estimating the effects of EC membership on trade. (NESC 1989). It is even more difficult to estimate the effects of membership on Irish social policy. Quite apart from the difficulties in establishing causal relationships, there is a serious shortage of research in relevant areas.

Since we cannot know what social policy changes would have occurred in the absence of EC membership, we have to look at what policy changes were required by the EC and what policy changes occurred without EC intervention. This also presents difficulties since changes may have come about because of the influence rather than the direct legal requirements of EC membership.

This paper looks at the legislative and administrative changes which were brought into the law, social policy and social services in Ireland because of EC membership. It also refers to the influence, usually unquantifiable, of EC practices, ideas etc. on national policies and services.

The main arguments put forward in this chapter are as follows:

- The EC has had a major influence on Irish social policy and services; much of that influence is difficult to quantify but it has been particularly influential in regard to the rights of women and of workers.

- Ireland has implemented nearly all the required social provisions – with the notable exception of equality in social welfare. That implementation has, however, always been minimal and has not included any attempt to address wider issues.

- Without EC membership it is unlikely that provisions such as equal pay and equal opportunity, consumer protection legislation and certain protective labour legislation would have been implemented when they were or at all. It is almost certain that equal treatment in social welfare would not have been implemented.

THE BACKGROUND

The Irish Context

In order to understand the impact of EC social policies on this country it is necessary first to look at what constitutes national social policy. In the national context, social policy objectives tend to be achieved by cash transfers, direct and indirect taxation, the provision of social services such as health, housing and education and the setting of minimum standards in various areas. Economic and agricultural policies very often tend to have social effects, whether accidental or intentional, but these are outside the scope of this paper.

There is relatively little serious discussion of social policy in the political world. The social consequences of, for example, taxation policy, are rarely analysed before implementation nor is there much analytical discussion of issues at government level. Indeed, it could be argued that there is no coherent overall policy but more a series of interventions to deal with specific problems and then correction for anomalies that arise from those interventions. NESC (1981) points out that:

> The development of Irish social policy in recent years has been characterised by pragmatic piecemeal reaction to perceived needs, often those advocated by organised interest groups. There has been relatively little consideration of the principles which should inform the rational development of social policy.

The Commission on Social Welfare report did provide a set of principles for the development of the social welfare system but these have never been totally accepted as government policy.

The debate on Ireland's accession to the EC was not greatly concerned with social policy. The government White Paper on *The Accession of Ireland to the European Communities* (1972) gives a few short paragraphs to the subject.

> The EEC Treaty requires the member states to implement the principle of equal pay for men and women. We would, of course, be considering the introduction of equal pay independently of our membership of the Community in the light of the recent recommendation by the Commission on the Status of Women that equal pay be implemented here in full by the end of 1977.
>
> The EEC Treaty does not specifically provide for the harmonisation of social security systems and, accordingly, membership of the Community will not impose any direct obligation on us to modify our system. However, as the treaty envisages, the operation of the Common Market will itself tend to bring about harmonisation of the social security systems of the member states.
>
> The resources of the European Social Fund will be available to us to assist in the expansion of our retraining and resettlement schemes.

Given the record of involvement by the EC in social policy issues at the time, this is not a surprising assessment of what EC membership meant in this area. Most of the major developments in EC social policy took place after Ireland's accession.

Scope of EC Social Policy

In assessing the impact of EC social policy on Ireland, the limited EC involvement in social areas must be recognised. The major impetus towards developing social policy at EC level has come from the recognition that economic policies have social costs. Because the impetus has come from economic policies, the concentration of activity has been on issues related to employment and unemployment. For instance, the Community is not involved in deciding on social welfare payments which is one of the most important social policy instruments available to national governments.

The EC is not involved in the direct provision of social services nor is it involved in deciding on who qualifies for those services. The EC has no role in direct taxation which is a significant element of any income distribution policy. While there are small programmes for specific groups e.g. the Poverty 3 programme, there is no direct EC input into policy for one parent families, child support, the elderly, housing. It has been suggested that the main aim of the smaller programmes is to increase public support for the EC. While they probably have that effect, and that may be a significant reason behind them, it must be recognised that they do have a major impact in raising awareness of the issues themselves.

THE EUROPEAN SOCIAL FUND

The European Social Fund (ESF) has been, and continues to be, particularly important to Ireland. In the five years to the end of 1993, Ireland will have received one billion pounds from the fund, which represents just over one third of all the money spent in Ireland in that period on vocational training and employment programmes. A significantly larger percentage of the labour force in Ireland benefits from the ESF than in any other member state – 18% of women and 13% of men have received ESF assistance in Ireland; the EC average is 2%. This is at least partly due to the large proportion of the Irish labour force which is aged under 25 and the emphasis which the rules of the fund places on this age group. There has been a huge expansion in financial outlay, in facilities, in training organisations and in numbers trained since 1973. The availability of ESF financing was largely, if not entirely, responsible for this.

The main objective of the programmes which are assisted by the ESF is to provide the skills needed to facilitate economic development and job creation. The fund also assists programmes to help the disadvantaged – the long-term unemployed, early school leavers, handicapped people and women returning to work. There are 15 separate agencies delivering training which is assisted by the ESF. Just over 150,000 people benefit each year.

There has been no systematic study of the use to which this money is put. Laffan's study (1985) is concerned with the defusion of expenditure among the major beneficiaries and the kinds of programmes being run but not with the nature and content of the programmes. She concludes that the ESF has been a major incentive to increasing the availability of training in Ireland but the main effect has been a quantitative one. The impact of the Community and on the kind and quality of manpower policies and programmes is minimal.

The availability of ESF financing meant that emphasis in training programmes was on youth unemployment – an area in which Ireland did have and continues to have a major problem. However, it also meant that less emphasis was placed on the needs of older unemployed workers. The National Planning Board stated in 1984 that it would be misguided to intensify the policies that discriminate in favour of young job seekers (National Planning Board report, 1984: 24).

An evaluation unit has only recently (January 1992) been established in the Department of Labour to examine the impact of expenditure on training and employment schemes. The Report of the Industrial Policy Review Group (1992 – the Culliton report) is very critical of the depth and quality of training schemes:

> ... about 90% of FÁS's budget goes on activities which are loosely classifiable as training, but fit better under the heading of unemployment support (p. 54).

Since a significant element of FÁS financing comes from the ESF it must be concluded that much of it is not going towards its intended target. In effect, the ESF has been providing support for the unemployed through the use of the fund for financing a social protection system rather than contributing to training which would lead to employment. While a cogent argument can be made for EC support for income maintenance for the unemployed, it remains the case that ESF funds should have been used for the purposes intended. The Culliton report is also critical of the influence of ESF criteria on those schemes :

> ... too much of the national training budget seems to be allocated by reference to the criteria for Structural Fund assistance from Brussels (p.55).

It would seem that Ireland is not alone in its approach to ESF funding. In *UK and EC Membership Evaluated* (1992), it is argued that the UK has used ESF funding to substitute for unemployment payments and has allowed ESF funding criteria to influence the design of benefit and training programmes.

The failure to have rigorous evaluation of EC funding is also addressed in the Culliton report:

> . . . we have also observed a widely held perception, in both the public and the private sectors, that the Structural Funds represent in some way 'free money from Brussels', the allocation of which requires to be less rigorously evaluated and accounted for than normal. The allocation of resources by Departments to the management of activities co-financed by the Structural Funds appears to be on the minimalist basis of ensuring that the draw down of funds is at the fastest possible level without sufficient attention to ensuring the most effective use of the funds (p. 49).

This criticism is aimed at all the Structural Funds but it would seem to be particularly applicable to the ESF. ESF financing has been available for certain courses in Regional Technical Colleges and similar institutions which has allowed for a considerable expansion in the numbers who avail of third level education. The availability of ESF grants was probably responsible for the greatly increased training facilities available to handicapped people since the mid-1970s. Faughnan and O'Connor (1980) point out that ESF assistance is primarily for projects and people geared towards open employment. They expressed concern that ESF support ". . . vital as it is for ongoing development, will not be the sole determinant of the direction which all vocational rehabilitation services will take". They were concerned that, if this happened, people who would not be capable of open employment, even after training and rehabilitation, would lose out.

Again, while there are certain obvious gains to handicapped people, there has been no assessment or evaluation of how the money has been spent, and whether or not it is meeting the real needs as distinct from the needs that fit ESF financing criteria. It is also suggested that for lack of alternative resources, ESF funding may have been used to train people who, by a strict interpretation, might not have had the appropriate criteria; the regulations in this area are being tightened up at present. There does not seem to be any alternative plan at national level for these people who, while they may not be in a position to meet ESF objectives, nevertheless would benefit from appropriate training. Overall, while ESF financing has unquestionably been a major benefit of EC membership it could have been even more beneficial if a greater emphasis was placed on the real needs of the people concerned and the schemes had been evaluated.

DISTRIBUTION OF INCOME

Although, the EC has no direct role in relation to taxation or eligibility for, or level of, cash benefits, it is worth exploring whether it has had any influence on the distribution of income.

Effects on Social Welfare Payments

As the White Paper on entry to the EC recognised, membership did not require that levels of social welfare payments be harmonised. However, it did require a measure of coordination for migrant workers which is referred to below. The level of payments has increased in real terms during the period of EC membership but there is no evidence to suggest that increases were awarded in order to bring Irish rates closer to the EC norm. It could be argued that the availability of EC funds released resources for use in improving social welfare payments and, therefore, EC membership was indirectly beneficial. It can also be argued that ESF funding of training services, in the main, has been support for the unemployed and thus has directly contributed to the income maintenance system.

Ireland had the highest growth rate in the EC in expenditure per head on social protection in the period 1970 -80 but, of course, we were starting from a low base. Much lower growth occurred in the 1980s in all countries except Greece. By 1989, Ireland's expenditure, in spite of considerable growth was 56% of the EC average. (RAPID Reports Population and social conditions 1991).

There continues to be considerable divergence in the financing of social expenditure: Ireland has the second lowest level of employer contributions and employee contributions and, not surprisingly, the second highest level of government contributions. (The trend of government contributions is, however, downward in Ireland).

The level of employer and employee contributions has significance not just for questions of social policy but also for competitiveness.

In discussion of these questions, Ireland's comparative position *vis-a-vis* other EC countries is often quoted but usually only to prove a point. There is little evidence that decisions are taken in order to bring us further into line with standards in other EC countries: decisions are usually taken on national budgetary considerations and not on EC issues. There are no EC requirements on these issues so there is no obligation on Ireland to move towards an EC standard. There seems to be little evidence that standards in other EC countries have much influence either.

The Social Welfare System

The Irish social welfare system is (and was in 1973) a mixture of insurance-based and means-tested payments. The relative importance of the two streams varies with time but, in EC terms, insurance is relatively unimportant. Means-tested payments in Ireland tend to be awarded on a household basis rather than on an individual basis. This creates enormous problems for the implementation of equality of treatment between the sexes.

When equality of treatment was finally implemented, a new provision was introduced which limited the amount of social welfare payments a married couple could receive where one or each was receiving unemployment assistance. This provision, which was not required by the Directive but was introduced for reasons of cost, was the subject of court proceedings and was found to be unconstitutional (Hyland v The Minister for Social Welfare). The government response was to extend the provision to cohabiting couples as well as married couples.

This, of course, is difficult to implement but gets over the constitutional difficulty. It means that the Irish system is moving further away from the EC aim restated in the EC Recommendation on Convergence, of emphasising individual rights and getting away from derived rights, i.e. the notion that people should be entitled to benefits in *their own* right and not as the spouse or dependant of someone else. In fact, it is notable that the Household Payments Review Group report (1991) did not even consider the issue of moving towards the EC aim of individual payments.

There has been a move away from providing more insurance based payments. The only new insurance based payment introduced since EC membership is the Deserted Wife's Benefit (1974). This is arguably not a suitable contingency for insurance payments anyway and, since April

1992, it is in the unusual position of being both means tested and insurance based. In fact, the likelihood is that it will be abolished within the next few years. All subsequent improvements for one parent families have involved means-tested payments. The Lone Parent Allowance scheme operates on the implicit assumption that the parents – almost all women – will stay at home and not seek employment. Schemes for lone parent families in other EC countries tend to operate on the basis that benefits would top up employment income rather than substitute for it.

Unemployment Assistance is now a much more important payment for the unemployed than is Unemployment Benefit. Pay related benefit was introduced in 1974 and has since been virtually abolished. The 1970's ubiquitous item in election manifestos – the national income related pension scheme – has been quietly forgotten about. There is now an acceptance that private pension arrangements are to be encouraged but with greater regulation. The national income related pension scheme idea – again, never officially dropped from the agenda – has been the victim of budgetary considerations and the British experience. There is nothing to suggest that the issue was in any way affected by EC trends.

These changes and policy shifts have been largely, if not entirely, due to national budgetary considerations. The issue of further divergence from EC standards is notable by its absence from the discussions on these issues.

Migrant Workers

The EC regulations on social security for migrant workers are now well established as described in Chapter 4. They effect large numbers of mobile workers amounting to more than 5 million. However, the provisions relating to pensions seem to be used more than the provisions relating to unemployment support. In spite of the fact that there is a high level of unemployment among migrant workers, many do not appear to claim their entitlement under the social security regulations. In 1990, only 312 people leaving Ireland exported their unemployment benefit to another EC country and only 96 brought their payments back to Ireland. This may be due to a combination of ignorance of the rules and the administrative difficulties involved. An unemployed person must have been receiving benefit in the country of last insurance for 4 weeks before transferring it to another country. The transferred payment is then only payable for 13 weeks.

The rules are fully implemented in Ireland. As with most EC legislation they set minimum standards only but there is nothing to stop particular countries improving on them. For example, under the rules unemployment benefit is payable to a person only by the country in which the last social insurance contribution was paid in respect of him or her. A citizen of another member state coming to Ireland, or an Irish citizen returning after working in another member state, has to have paid at least one contribution here before being qualified to receive unemployment benefit. The EC regulations do not require the Irish government to restrict eligibility in this way but they do not prevent them from doing so either. Attempts have been made on a number of occasions to change this particular rule at EC level, but so far without success.

Pensioners who have worked in another member state do seem to make use of the regulations. Half of the pensions paid to pensioners living overseas by the UK Department of Social Security are paid to people living in Ireland, but these rights existed before EC membership.

Health Services

The EC is involved in health services policy only in specific and limited ways, mainly health promotion on cancer and AIDS. The programmes involved are mainly for coordinating national activities. *The Europe against Cancer* programme introduced an innovatory policy of collaboration on health promotion. Ireland has had a leading role in relation to cancer and the control of tobacco advertising. This health promotion activity was already under way in Ireland before the Europe against Cancer programmes started but undoubtedly benefited from the collaboration with other member states.

The level of health service provision, and the extent of entitlement to free services, have been almost entirely in the hands of the Irish government and have been virtually unaffected by EC policies. Membership of the EC can be said to have affected policy only indirectly e.g. by releasing resources from other areas.

The proportion of household expenditure going towards health care is lower in Ireland than in any other EC member state – 1.5% of the household budget goes on health services in Ireland compared with an EC average of 3.2% and 4.8% (the highest percentage) in France.

Entitlement to free health services has changed very little since EC entry, with the exception of the change in June 1979 which gave everyone entitlement to a free public bed, and the further change in June 1991 which extended entitlement to free consultants' services to the whole population. About 15% of the population had not had these entitlements but the evidence of increasing VHI membership would suggest that very few of that percentage avail themselves of their new entitlements. The proportion of the population covered by medical cards has declined in recent years: this is due to cutbacks in the health service budget and is not affected by EC considerations. A significant section of the population chooses to use private care and is insured to do so. The EC has not yet affected the virtual monopoly position of the VHI but will do so from July 1994 when the 3rd Non-Life Insurance Directive (Directive 92/49/EEC) comes into effect. This Directive will allow the Irish government to make it mandatory for other insurers entering the Irish market to offer community rating and life membership. If the Government were to exercise this option, it would mean that the VHI will no longer be the only insurer although there will be no change in the standard of health insurance available.

It is still true to say that the EC has a limited competence in the whole area of health. The Maastricht Treaty would give the Community specific competence in the public health area including the prevention of major diseases, promotion of research, health information and education. However, the emphasis on subsidiarity may mean that there will be little real change and it is highly unlikely that there will be EC Directives on entitlement or access to services.

Housing

The area of housing policy has also been virtually unaffected by EC membership, except, possibly, for the freeing of resources argument.

Social Europe No. 2/92 clearly outlines the lack of EC competence in the area. The traditionally high level of owner occupation, and the state support for it, have not been affected. There have been some moves in recent years to put homelessness on the EC agenda and this is referred to below.

EQUALITY BETWEEN MEN AND WOMEN

Without EC membership, it is highly unlikely (despite what is stated in the White Paper) that equal pay and equal treatment legislation would have reached the statute books when they did. In fact, it is possible that this might never have happened without EC intervention. The government and employers' organisations lobbied for derogation from implementation of the Equal Pay Directive. It was implemented in spite of this.

The continued monitoring of the equality legislation by the EC Commission and the recourse to the European Court of Justice has meant that the legislation has had to be interpreted and implemented in a broader way than would have happened if the context was purely Irish.

It is generally considered that EC membership has been good for women and this is undoubtedly true. Particularly for women in employment. A report of the Joint Committee on Secondary legislation of the EC (1984) stated:

> The Community has brought about changes in employment practices which might otherwise have taken decades to achieve. Irish women have the Community to thank for the removal of the marriage bar in employment, the introduction of maternity leave, greater opportunities to train at a skilled trade, protection against dismissal on pregnancy, the disappearance of advertisements specifying the sex of an applicant for a job and greater equality in the social welfare code. After farmers, Irish women in employment have probably benefited most from entry to the EEC.

While the general thrust of this statement is correct, it attributes more change to the EC than was actually the case. The introduction of maternity leave and the protection against dismissal on pregnancy did not result from EC requirements. Membership of the EC probably did contribute to the political willingness to improve the rights of women in employment. There can be little doubt that it contributed, in ways that are impossible to quantify, to a general change in attitude towards women's rights. Women's organisations have built up contacts and generally made good use of the EC Networks etc. thereby contributing to consciousness-raising. In spite of this, the position of women workers in Ireland is not good. Without EC membership it would be worse.

Participation in the labour force by married women remains low by EC standards – in 1987, 35.1% of married women in Ireland were active in the labour force while the level was 56.1% in the EC as a whole. (Statistical Office of EC, 1989).

The NESC report on Women's Participation in the Irish Labour Market (1991) shows that, *inter alia*, while the participation rates of women have increased they are still significantly lower than in most developed countries and there is high persistent occupational segregation between men and women. Pyle (1990) has argued that government policy played a decisive role in ensuring that men had priority in the labour market.

Childcare facilities are relatively undeveloped in Ireland. The link between availability of childcare and participation in the labour force is obvious (and is recognised in NESC report No. 91) – Denmark has the highest level of publicly-financed childcare provision in the EC and also has the highest participation rate for women with children under the age of 5. Ireland and the UK are the lowest in both.

Legislation alone will not eliminate inequality. The equal pay and equal opportunity legislation in any event is largely of benefit to women in employment. There is no government policy of promoting employment for women and, as is pointed out above, social welfare payments for lone parents tend to militate against employment. There has been very little political commitment to promoting the participation of women – in 1989 some member states , including Ireland, said in response to an EC questionnaire that they did not feel it necessary to adopt specific measures to combat female unemployment. The ratio of women's earnings to those of men increased in the 1970s but there has been little or no change in the 80s; the ratio in Ireland is among the lowest in Europe but broadly in line with the UK. An expert on the issue has noted that "the data that would enable the effective monitoring of equal treatment legislation to take place are not collected which itself suggests that equal treatment has not been made a priority" (Blackwell, 1990). Participation by women in the EC programmes for young people has been high. More women than men took part in the ERASMUS scheme in 1987/88 (54% were women) and Ireland had the highest female participation rate (71% of Irish participants were female). About 50% of participants on Youth Exchange programmes are women but in the technological exchange programme – COMETT – only about 33% were women.

In 1989, 1.4% of top managers were women and only one third of companies had women at middle management level.

Overall, although the position of women is still very much short of equality, it must be said that EC membership has been good for women.

Women in Agriculture and the Self-Employed

No attempt has been made to address the issues arising from Council Directive 86/613/EEC on the application of the principle of equal treatment between men and women engaged in an activity including agriculture, in a self-employed capacity, and on the protection of self-employed women during pregnancy and motherhood. Most parts of the Directive do not require any special legislative measures but the government do not seem to have done anything about those provisions which suggest that certain aspects be examined. This provides another example of the minimalist approach to Directives and of the unwillingness to do anything that is not specifically required. Ireland would seem to be in breach of one aspect of the Directive and the Department of Social Welfare has accepted that this is so. Among other things, this Directive requires that the spouses of self-employed who participate in the activities of the self-employed person be allowed to join a social security scheme. This would affect many women married to farmers and shopkeepers. At present, such spouses may only pay self-employed PRSI if they are partners in the activity.

Equal Treatment in Social Welfare

It can be argued that the implementation in Ireland of the EC Directive on equality of treatment for men and women in social security does not reflect well on most of the participants. In spite of having six years to prepare, the date for implementation passed without any action by the government. The method of implementation which was finally decided upon was, in some respects, discriminatory and the government has been accused of being negligent in its handling of this issue. There were difficulties to be overcome but that is precisely why a longer than normal time was given to governments to implement this Directive. During the six years for preparation, and particularly in 1981/82, there were substantial increases in social welfare payments generally. The opportunity could have been taken to change the rules on dependency at that time – at little cost to the exchequer or to the people affected.

Equality has a price and most Irish people affected by the Directive were not prepared to pay the price. The so-called "compensating payments" which were introduced to quell the outcry resulting from the loss of benefits by married men were themselves discriminatory. Following a decision of the European Court of Justice, the Government was obliged to pay retrospective payments to the women affected by the failure to implement the Directive.

The general direction of EC policy in this area is towards individual rights and away from derived rights. Yet, in recent years, the Irish social welfare system has moved more towards household payments, notably in the restrictions on amounts payable to married couples and to cohabiting couples. These restrictions mean that there is not much point in a married woman applying for certain payments in her own right. This then means that she does not get credited social insurance contributions which means that she will not have entitlement in her own right to pensions and other benefits.

Unemployed women and their representatives claim that some women are still asked questions on childcare arrangements when applying for Unemployment Benefit or Unemployment Assistance in spite of memorandums from the Department of Social Welfare with contrary instructions. This is the sort of covert discrimination which legislation of itself will not eliminate but which requires action at national level.

There is an EC Recommendation on positive action (1984) which includes giving positive action a place in collective bargaining. There is no evidence that this was taken on board by either the government or the social partners.

WORKERS' RIGHTS

Some of the major improvements in statutory protection for workers since 1973 e.g. the Unfair Dismissals Act, Maternity (Protection of Employees) Act, were not due to EC membership. Improved protection for part-time workers was introduced in 1991 ahead of the EC proposals in the area. There were a number of other protective labour laws which were necessitated by EC membership.

Rights of Part-Time Workers

Until April 1991, employees who worked for less than 18 hours a week were, generally speaking, excluded from social insurance coverage and from protective labour legislation. There were a number of cases before the ECJ which suggested that such exclusion could be contrary to the Equal Pay and Opportunities Directives. There are proposals for Directives under the Social Charter Implementation Programme. These are being introduced not just for social reasons but also (perhaps mainly) to ensure competitiveness.

In Ireland, legislation was introduced before agreement was reached on the proposed Directives. There are problems with its social insurance aspects. The protective labour legislation is fully in accord with the proposed EC Directive.

Social insurance coverage was extended to part-time workers who earn over £25 a week from April 1991. The proposed EC Directive would extend social insurance to people who work at least 8 hours a week. When the £25 a week proposal was being discussed in the Dail, there was virtually no reference to the fact that it was out of line with the EC proposals.

The Worker Protection (Part-Time Employees) Act 1990 meets all the requirements of the proposed EC Directive with regard to protective legislation and, in fact, goes further. It does not deal, however, with areas such as rights to company training and seniority pay which are covered in the proposed Directive.

Minimum Standards: Health and Safety

The EC has brought about a considerable improvement in the legislation on standards for health and safety in the workplace. This has been the case particularly since the Single European Act and the use of qualified majority voting under Article 118A. It is also the case that standards of health and safety at work are easier to harmonise than standards in almost every other social policy area. The Safety, Health and Welfare at Work Act 1989 set up the National Authority for Occupational Safety and Health.

The Authority should be in a position to implement the EC Framework Directive and the other Directives arising from it.

The view of the UK Health and Safety Commission (1989) also reflects the Irish situation:

> The EC is in effect emerging as the main engine of law-making in safety and health, principally as regards major health hazards and the risks posed by very dangerous and toxic substances, but now also in an approach to regulating more traditional workplace hazards and to influencing workplace institutions . . . We propose to recognise that henceforth the European programme will represent the overwhelming share of our legislative effort.

Having the legislation in place is only one aspect of safety and health at work. Whether that legislation is adequately administered and policed is a separate issue and purely in the hands of the Irish government.

Employment Crises: Employees' Rights

The Protection of Employees (Employers' Insolvency) Act 1984 implemented Council Directive 80/987 EEC which provides for various protective measures for workers affected by the insolvency of their employer. This has been a direct benefit to those workers whose employers have become insolvent and owing money to the workers in the form of unpaid wages, pension contributions, minimum notice entitlements etc. In 1990, there were approximately 2,400 employees who claimed entitlements (there were 284 insolvent employers involved). £2.9m was paid out and £750,000 recovered. (Annual Report of the Department of Labour).

The Protection of Employment Act 1977 implemented Directive 75/129/EEC which sets out a system of notification and consultation in the event of collective redundancies. There were 74 collective redundancies notified during 1990 – these affected 6,139 employees. It is doubtful if these measures contributed much to the well-being of workers as there is no evidence to suggest that prior warning of redundancies has any effect on the final outcome. The first time a penalty was imposed on an employer for failure to comply with the Act was in October 1992. The fine was £50 which hardly constitutes a disincentive. It is generally accepted that there are defects and problems with the original Directive and some of these are being addressed in a proposed amended Directive.

The Commission has been critical of the implementation of the collective redundancies directive. Its Report to the Council (1991) points out that there "appears to be a number of ways in which Irish law may not be fully in line with the aims and procedures set down in the Directive". It also points out that the Directive was implemented after the due date.

The EC (Safeguarding of Employees Rights on Transfer of Undertakings) Regulations 1980 implemented Directive 77/187/EEC which deals with employees' rights in the event of a transfer of the business (the "acquired rights" Directive). The Commission report to the Council on the implementation of the Directive (1992) makes several criticisms of the Irish legislation. It notes that the scope of the legislation is unclear, that the wording is transposed directly from the Directive without defining the concepts involved, that the opportunity to extend it was not availed of and the manner in which the question of employees' representatives is handled is unsatisfactory. Prondzynski and McCarthy had already expressed similar criticisms. They note that the exact wording of the Directive was used and some of these words do not have real meaning in an Irish context; they question the use of a Statutory Instrument to bring it into effect and they generally regard this legislation and the Protection of Employees Act as inadequate.

PROGRAMMES FOR SPECIFIC GROUPS

Anti-poverty programmes, programmes for the disabled etc., were never designed to deal with all the relevant problems. They were always seen at EC level as ancillary to national government activity. In Ireland, they have often not been accompanied by real government action. The major impact of these programmes is not really in the direct aid provided but in their roles as vehicles for exchange of information and experience and in raising awareness of the issues involved. Poverty is seen as primarily a problem for the member states. The EC poverty programmes are limited in intention but they, nevertheless, have had considerable impact. The 2nd European Poverty Programme was designed to help member states with their anti-poverty programme; it aimed to propose innovative and universally applicable measures based on field trials and to cast light on the causes of poverty.

The Final Report on the 2nd European Poverty Programme 1985-89 (COM 91/29) concluded that projects demonstrate the importance of developing national income support policies and the need to guarantee resources; to adapt national employment and vocational training policies to take account of the least privileged groups. It also noted that "as project scopes were limited, it is not possible to evaluate their effects in terms of reducing the number of particularly deprived unemployed persons in the project area" The projects showed up institutional obstacles in social protection systems and the universal need for potential beneficiaries to be informed and advised.

The 2nd Poverty Programme in Ireland led to the establishment of the Community Development Programme by the Department of Social Welfare. This happened more or less by accident in that some form of funding was needed for those groups who had been funded by the Poverty Programme and who had no source of income when that programme ended. This programme exists alongside a scheme of grants for voluntary organisations, another scheme for women's organisations and a system of once-off annual grants to voluntary organisations for specific projects.

These schemes are unquestionably all useful worthwhile schemes and are almost all concerned with empowering people in their local communities as well as with what might be termed conventional anti-poverty activities. However, none of these schemes has a legislative base nor any published criteria for the award of grants.

The 3rd Poverty Programme is currently in progress. In Ireland, it involves three projects. It is not yet possible to attempt any assessment of its impact.

Programmes for the disabled are also limited in scope. The disabled in Ireland do benefit from specific ESF funding for vocational training as well as from the specific programmes – Horizon (this is for the socially disadvantaged and not simply the disabled in the traditional sense) and Helios.

There are also very small programmes for groups such as the elderly and travellers. These have not been in existence for long enough for an assessment of their effectiveness to be made.

Overall, the Culliton report was critical of the many small programmes financed by the Structural Funds – "too many minor initiatives, heavy in administrative bureaucracy but light in economic impact, appear to be co-financed under the Funds". Local Community groups who have benefited under these schemes would not agree with this assessment. It has been argued that some of these schemes have been brought into existence to redress the exclusion of disadvantaged groups from the planing of the National Development Plan (Rafferty in *Poverty Today*, Oct/Dec 1992).

INDIRECT INFLUENCES ON POLICY

There can be little doubt that thinking on social policy, expectations etc. have been affected by EC membership. Policymakers and pressure groups at national level are all exposed to EC influences either at official level or through international lobbying organisations.

The Commission has set up a huge range of committees, working groups and observatories to monitor policies, collect information and exchange experiences. These involve people from government, academic life, pressure groups, trade unions and employers and have a major role in promoting exchanges of information and experience. Ireland partakes fully in these activities and policies must be affected by what is learned there. The importance of the availability of information cannot be overstated as it enables pressure groups to advance their case by using comparative data from other member states. It is the sort of influence which is impossible to quantify but which is unquestionably very important. Arguments in favour of better child care provisions are almost always based on EC comparisons. Overall, this is the sort of influence that cannot be quantified or proven but it is arguably even more important than much of the legislation.

The European Parliament's role is less influential but there is evidence to suggest that their recommendations are taken into account. There is also some evidence that discussions at the Parliament can cause embarrassment to member states. For example, when bringing in legislation to repeal the vagrancy laws, the Minister for Justice cited a European Parliament report which castigated Ireland's laws as one of the influences which brought about his decision.

The involvement of non-governmental organisations (NGOs) in the delivery of social services is one aspect of the Irish system which differs considerably from other member states. The increasing importance of the EC to their activities is obvious from the degree to which Irish NGOs have become involved in the lobbying and consultative processes in Brussels. Irish groups working for the homeless were very active in setting up a European grouping (FEANTSA) which has now managed to get homelessness on to the EC agenda. Similarly, Irish groups were to the fore in setting up the European Anti-Poverty Network.

European organisations for the disabled and the elderly are also active and there are Irish organisations involved. The funding of voluntary organisations through initiatives such as Horizon and NOW is a novel development which could prove to have major repercussions for the provision of social services and for the enhancement of the power of the voluntary sector.

6. FURTHER EC INTEGRATION AND SOCIAL POLICY

Larry Bond

From here on, in this volume we look towards the future. Are the problems which social policy has to address likely to increase or decrease? What responses do we need, and what responses are we likely to get, at EC level and in Ireland? In this chapter, we begin by considering the likely effects of the Single European Market (SEM) and Economic and Monetary Union (EMU). The prospects for the future developments of the EC "Social Dimension" are also considered.

The Effects of the SEM and EMU

The main findings of the Commission's research programme on the effects of the Single Market are well known. Using a combination of approaches they estimate that the Single Market programme would increase GDP by between 4.5 per cent and 7 per cent, and could add 1.8 to 5.0 million jobs to the Community total (Emerson *et al*, 1988, p. 218). The Commission authors emphasise the difficulties inherent in making these kinds of forecasts, and present their findings as broad indicators:

> any estimates of the effects of a complex action like completing the internal market can only be regarded as very approximate. Apart from being subject to a number of policy conditions, such estimates are extremely difficult to make, especially as regards some of the more speculative and long-term effects (*ibid.*, p.3).

Not surprisingly, the Commission estimates have been widely debated. On the optimistic side, it has been suggested that the likely benefits of the Single Market could be significantly greater than those estimated. Baldwin (1989) suggests that the 'growth bonus' arising from the dynamic effects of the Single Market on investment and innovation has been underestimated. He suggests that these dynamic effects could be significantly greater than the static benefits estimated by the Commission.

On the opposite side of the argument are those who suggest that the benefits of the Single Market have been overestimated (Cutler *et al*, 1989; Thompson, 1991). According to these authors, many of the assumptions built into the Commission estimates reflect over-optimistic readings of often patchy data. Thompson specifically argues that this is the case with regard to the size and significance of potential economies of scale. It is also suggested that the Commission estimates underplay the likely significance of the 'policy conditions' to which they are subject. While the complete elimination of non-tariff barriers is assumed, critics suggest that partial elimination to a greater or less extent is probably a more realistic assumption. The more optimistic forecasts also assume the adoption of complementary macroeconomic policies ('a cooperative growth strategy') though in the past, at least, this has proved difficult to achieve for any significant period.

In addition, critics argued that the estimates of potential gains rely on unrealistic assumptions about the significance of the barriers targeted for removal as part of the Single Market programme (Grahl and Teague, 1990; Teague 1991). The 'fragmentation' of European markets is not simply a result of administrative barriers but is a result of different national and regional histories, cultures and institutions and is, therefore, likely to persist or, at best, to change relatively slowly. Overall, these critical arguments suggest, in Thomson's words, an attitude of "healthy scepticism of the officially calculated benefits". Just as important, they challenge the emphasis on market liberalisation as the primary route to gains from integration. Rather meaningful integration will require more developed economic institutions and greater coordination of policies at a European level.

Economic and Monetary Union would involve the coordination of economic policy at the Community level. However, the version of the EMU in the Maastricht Treaty concentrates on monetary union (setting up of a European Central Bank and the eventual introduction of common currency). Consideration of broader economic policy is narrowly focused, concentrating on the controls on fiscal policy seen as necessary to achieve the monetary objectives. In Commission research, it has been estimated that the direct effects of monetary union, through reduced transaction costs, the elimination of exchange rate uncertainty and lower interest rates, are likely to be beneficial for the Community economy as a whole (Emerson and Huhne, 1991). Overall, the size and timing of the effects of EMU are unclear. Again, this optimistic conclusion has been challenged (Mason, Symmetry, 1992; Minford *et al.* 1992).

Even then not all member states may participate. Some of the expected benefits may arise in the transitional period as we move towards EMU. Against this, the convergence conditions that must be achieved as a condition of establishing the EMU may have deflationary effects which will work against the achievement of growth in the Community in the 1990s. More generally, the formation of a monetary union and institutions whose focus is the achievement of price stability seems likely to introduce a deflationary bias into European policy-making in the absence of matching economic institutions and measures focused on growth. The obstacles to the successful coordination of economic policies, in the absence of more developed institutions at European level, has highlighted the divergent national policies pursued by the major Community countries in recent years and indeed in recent months. Community growth performance in the 1980s also benefited significantly from strong growth in the rest of the world economy which is likely to be weaker in this decade. To make any significant impact on unemployment in the Community by the end of the decade, a growth performance that is somewhat better than that achieved in the 1980s will be required. How growth on this scale might be achieved is far from clear.

IMPACT ON IRELAND

The Commission studies have been most heavily criticised for failing to consider the likely regional distribution of the benefits of integration. The Commission studies suggested (where they considered the matter at all) that the benefits would be evenly spread, or even that they would favour smaller and newer member states. In a major study of Ireland's EC membership, the National Economic and Social Council (NESC, 1989) argued that the benefits are more likely to be unevenly distributed in favour of the core regions.

However, the NESC report did not attempt to quantify likely effects. A subsequent study suggested that the Irish economy stands to gain in the long run from 1992 but that "The overall economic benefits are less than those estimated for the EC as a whole in the Cecchini report as far as the major macroeconomic variables are concerned both in the short and the medium term" (Bradley, Fitzgerald and McCoy, 1991). This suggests that the Single Market alone would widen regional disparities in the Community at least with regard to Ireland. However, the effects of other policy changes accompanying the Single Market, especially increased Structural Fund expenditure, must also be taken into account.

This analysis has recently been further developed. Bradley *et al* (1992) estimate the likely impact on Ireland of a range of Community policies. They estimate that, together, the Single Market and increases in Structural Fund spending introduced in 1989-1993, will increase the average growth rate over the decade by 0.75 per cent. As a result GNP in the year 2000 will be 7 to 8 percentage points higher than it would be in the absence of these measures. They estimate EMU will also have a positive effect, possibly adding a further percentage point to output in the medium term.

However, CAP reform will probably have a negative effect, reducing output by 1-1.5 per cent in the longer term. It is estimated that taken together, these changes will add 55,000 to total employment by the end of the decade. This would reduce unemployment by around 25,000, the rest being accounted for by increases in the labour force brought about by reduced emigration. This study suggests that Ireland's growth increases will in absolute terms match those of the Community as a whole. However, the per capita increase will be lower as a result of the increase in population brought about by reduced emigration. These estimates of the impact of the Structural Funds do not take into account the increase in funds under the Delors II package. These increases should add to the impact on growth and employment.

Bradley *et al's* figures represent the best estimates available of the overall impact on Ireland of the changes taking place in the EC. Nonetheless, they must be treated with some caution. As the authors specifically highlight, estimating the supply side effects of structural spending (i.e. to what extent the productive capacity of the economy is enhanced on an ongoing basis as a result of the Structural Funds) is a very difficult exercise, whose results must be treated tentatively. The estimated impact of EMU also assumes that a considerable part of the expected benefits accrue in the transition period, i.e. before the EMU is actually adopted. Similarly, the final impact of CAP depends on the shape of the actual reforms that are eventually introduced. Finally, in estimating the effects of the Single Market on Ireland, the Commission's estimates for growth in the Community as a whole provide the base on which the Irish estimates are built. In so far as the reservations expressed above regarding the Commission estimates hold, they must also be applied to these Irish estimates.

We must also look beneath these aggregate estimates to the underlying processes in the economy. The NESC report emphasised that the most significant effects of integration to date have been on structural change in the Irish economy. Indigenous manufacturing fared particularly poorly as a result of integration. It suggests that a process of constant attrition has become established – "instead of integration stimulating dominant indigenous firms to exploit economies of scale and thus eliminate the tail of high cost producers, larger Irish manufactures would seem to have been part of the tail eliminated by producers in other countries" (p.160). Integration has exposed (as distinct from caused) the weakness of indigenous industry in particular. This underlying structural weakness is a large part of the explanation of our poor job-creation record. Further integration is likely to result in further attrition of indigenous industry unless successful countervailing policies are adopted at national and Community level.

SOCIAL POLICY

While successful economic policy is a necessary condition for social progress in Europe, it is by no means sufficient and must be matched by more developed social policies at both national and EC level. The idea that any further moves towards a European Union will require an enlarged social dimension has been promoted by some European leaders (notably Francois Mitterrand) since the early 1980s. The European Council at its Madrid meeting in June 1989 agreed that "in the course of the construction of the single European market social aspects should be given the same importance as economic aspects and should accordingly be developed in a balanced fashion". However, the actual development of EC social policies to date has been very limited(see Chapter 1).

EC social policy has been predominantly regulatory rather than redistributive and has been mainly, though not exclusively, concerned with the labour market rather than the wider welfare state. The Community does have some major mechanisms of redistribution on the CAP and the Structural Funds. However, spending in these areas is not guided predominantly by social policy concerns and may, from the social point of view, seem at times perverse.

In fact, there are fundamental political differences on the nature of the social dimension, which have resulted in considerable conflict within the Community. The British government has opposed most aspects of the social dimensions. For Britain "the real social dimension of the Single Market is the opportunity it will generate to create jobs and reduce unemployment to stimulate growth and prosperity and to improve living standards. Far from creating jobs, introduction of future measures as envisaged by the (Social) Charter would hamper job creation" quoted in Deakin and Wilkinson.

Britain was unique in Europe in the 1980s in having a Government for whom anti-trade unionism and deregulation of markets were articles of faith. Government policy in Britain has sought to restrict trade unions and employment rights more generally "as part of a wider strategy to increase the power of employers and strengthen managerial control in industrial relations *as a means of promoting greater efficiency and productivity in the economy*" (Wedderburn, 1991, p. 77, emphasis added). Thatcherism is a strong version of a more generally shared neo-liberal outlook for which equity and efficiency are mutually exclusive. On this view the growth of the welfare state has strangled the productive economy in Europe and wholesale deregulation is prescribed as the necessary antidote to 'Eurosclerosis'.

Neo-liberalism held centre stage in Britain throughout the 1980s but it had less success in the rest of Europe. Much of the European experience seems to contradict the neo-liberal story – "West Germany and Sweden are high wage economies with sticky wages; a low wage spread between industries, regions and categories of firms; long-term stable employment relationships based on legislation and centralised collective bargaining; and powerful trade unions exercising established rights to co-determination. Although these thoroughly 'Eurosclerotic' conditions have not markedly weakened in recent years and some have in fact gained in strength since the mid-1970s . . . both countries are undoubtedly highly competitive in world markets." (Streeck). Furthermore, it can be argued that the features of society derided by neo-liberals may be essential factors in the economic success of these countries by improving the quality of the workforce, defusing social conflicts and facilitating adjustment.

However, the ascendancy of neo-liberalism in the 1980s was not the only factor holding back the development of social policy. The Community has generally pursued political ends through economic means in order to minimise or sidestep conflict over fundamental political questions concerning sovereignty and political union. The issue of the further development of social policy at a Community level and, in particular, any development of major socially redistributive mechanisms impinges directly on these political concerns. It is an issue that has been largely avoided precisely for this reason.

Despite the removal of Mrs Thatcher herself, it is likely that Britain will continue to strongly resist the development of social policies at European level. It has also been suggested that the Britain against the rest scenario has meant that it has been easy for 'the rest' to exaggerate their commitment to the social dimension because there was no real chance of having to back the sentiment with (perhaps costly) action (Lange, 1992). Thus, the real level of support for greater social development of the Community is hard to judge. The general approach of the Social Charter and Action Programme (and now the Maastricht Agreement on Social Policy) has been mildly social protectionist, seeking the extension of a minimum floor of rights throughout the Community. While one can expect to see some extension of this approach in the coming years, there is no enthusiasm in the Community for the development of significant redistributive social policies as distinct from the mainly regulatory policies seen to date. In the absence of significant political shifts in the Community, there seems little likelihood of major changes in this picture in the foreseeable future.

Concluding Comments

In the 1980s, the main response to stagnation in the Community was the Single Market programme followed more recently with the moves towards Economic and Monetary Union set out in the Maastricht Treaty. This response has two major flaws. The first flaw is that the Single Market has clearly not created sustained growth. Thus, there remains a need for new approaches to encouraging economic development across the Community. The second flaw is that the approach has been predominantly a free market one without any real balancing concern for social development.

The Community has yet to develop comprehensive social policies alongside its economic role. To date, the general approach has been mildly "social protectionist", seeking the extension of a minimum floor of human rights throughout the Community for the development of redistributive social policies.

It must be increasingly a responsibility of the Community to ensure that there is a clear balance between economic and social development in the interests of all citizens. This was recognised to some extent on the agreement at Maastricht with the emphasis in the social protocol on "combating social exclusion" and "the integration of persons excluded from the labour market". The immediate challenge is to build on this recognition in the spending of the next round of the Structural Funds. In the longer term, the commitment to building a social as well as economic Europe seems unlikely to come about through behind-the-scenes-diplomacy. A major political initiative is required to raise the question of the future model of Europe within the Community institutions and in each of the member states.

7. TOWARDS CONVERGENCE OF SOCIAL PROTECTION SYSTEMS

Gerry Mangan

As we saw in Chapter 4, the EC's policies in the field of social protection have been limited in scope, dealing mainly with persons moving within the Community and questions of equality between men and women. In recent years, there is a new approach at EC level which involves actively promoting the convergence of member states' systems of social protection. In this chapter, the evolution and the main features of this policy are described. Convergence means the gradual and voluntary drawing together of different systems: it must be distinguished from the EC notion of harmonisation which means the compulsory adoption of elements of a common system. Harmonisation was an earlier option and is dealt with here first. The chapter concludes with a discussion of the main issues which member states face in adapting their systems to deal with the major social changes facing them.

HARMONISATION UNDER THE TREATY OF ROME

In the lead up to the Treaty of Rome in 1957, the need for the progressive harmonisation of social protection systems in parallel with the removal of customs barriers was discussed. The aim of this process would be to avoid a situation where countries with high levels of social protection would be at a competitive disadvantage compared to countries where the level of social protection was significantly lower, thus leading to a lowering of standards generally. In the event, however, it was felt that the need for harmonisation on these grounds was not compelling as the cost of social protection is just one factor determining competitiveness and could be outweighed by other factors which would enhance a country's competitiveness. This has been borne out to date by the fact that the more economically successful countries in the EC also have the highest levels of social protection.

The difficulties involved in attempting to harmonise systems which were so different was also a major consideration.

No specific provision, therefore, was made in the Treaty of Rome which would make progressive harmonisation of social protection systems mandatory, but it was envisaged that harmonisation could take place as a consequence of the functioning of the Common Market. This was referred to in Article 117 of the treaty as follows:

> Member States agree upon the need to promote improved working conditions and an improved standard of living for workers, so as to make possible their harmonisation while the improvement is being maintained.
>
> They believe that such a development will ensue not only from the functioning of the common market, which will favour the harmonisation of social systems, but also from the procedures provided for in this Treaty and from the approximation of provisions laid down by law, regulation or administrative action.

Article 117 envisaged that upward harmonisation would occur, and that it would occur in part at least from the functioning of the Common Market. This would appear to reflect the positive context for the development of systems of social protection (referred to in Chapter 3) which obtained in the post-war period up to the 1970s. Systems of social protection did develop significantly in that period, until the first oil crisis began the serious economic difficulties for all member states which are still with us. Since then, development has continued but at a much slower pace. However, spontaneous harmonisation of systems did not occur to any significant degree and individual member states have to a large extent gone their own way in developing their systems in accordance with their own history, culture and traditions.

Article 117 states that progress towards harmonisation would also be achieved "from the procedures provided for in the Treaty and from the approximation of provisions laid down by law, regulation or administrative action". In the field of social protection, the main areas where EC legislation has applied has been in relation to coordination and equal treatment referred to above (Chapter 4). The process of co-ordination does not appear to have contributed significantly to the harmonisation of social protection systems as the aim has mainly been to accommodate differences between the national systems, rather than getting national systems to change in order to facilitate coordination. Application of the principle of equal treatment has resulted in harmonisation in certain areas but the fundamental structures of the systems have not been changed.

It was also envisaged that harmonisation would occur through a process of consultation and research, for which Article 118 of the treaty provides a basis as follows:

> Without prejudice to the other provisions of this Treaty and in conformity with its general objectives, the Commission shall have the task of promoting close co-operation between the Member States in the social field, particularly in matters relating to . . . social security.
>
> To this end, the Commission shall act in close contact with Member States by making studies, delivering opinions and arranging consultations both on problems arising at national level and on those of concern to international organisations . . .

On the basis of Article 118, the EC Commission arranged for:

the exchange of information on developments in the area of social protection in Member States, through the regular publication of comparative tables on social security;

the development of quantitative analyses (social security budgets, medium-term social security projections, etc.);

regular exchanges on policies and systems in the framework of a consultation group composed of the Directors General (Permanent Secretaries) of Social Security Departments in the Member States and Commission officials.

It is difficult to establish the extent to which these activities had a real influence on the evolution of policy at national level in relation to social protection and, as a consequence, led to any greater harmonisation of systems between member states. However, as the positive context in which systems of social protection had developed began to change radically, especially from the late 1970s onwards, there was much greater interest in exchanging views and experiences on the best approaches to adopt in tackling, in particular, the problems of rising unemployment and the burdens and strains being placed on systems of social protection by social and demographic changes.

Two Commission Communications [Com(82)716 and Com(86)410] on developments in the field of social protection, with particular reference to the social, economic and demographic changes taking place, formed the basis for discussion on policy at informal meetings of Ministers with responsibility for social security in 1983 and 1987.

EVOLUTION OF POLICY OF CONVERGENCE

The Hazards of Integration

In the late 1980s, the potential negative impact on economic competitiveness of the increasing burden of financing social protection became of much greater concern in the context of progress towards the Single Market in 1992, and the prospect of even further economic integration, associated with Economic and Monetary Union. Until 1992, member states have been in a position to avoid the full rigours of competition by placing barriers in the way of importing goods and services from other countries. Completion of the Single Market required that these barriers had to be removed. If and when EMU is achieved, restoring competitiveness through devaluation of the national currency will not be an option. One of the major remaining areas where member states retain control is that of expenditure on social protection. The concern is, therefore, that member states may resort to what has come to be termed 'social devaluation', reducing expenditure on social protection in real terms to maintain competitiveness. If this approach were to be adopted generally by member states, it could result in existing systems of social protection being seriously undermined.

It is also being recognised that the disparities between systems of social protection may have a significant distorting effect on the mobility of persons within the Community. Workers will be reluctant to move or return to a country where the levels of social protection are not comparable to those obtaining in the country where they have been residing. Accordingly, countries with less developed systems of social protection may find it difficult to attract and retain the more highly trained and skilled workers. At a time of high unemployment, it is also more likely that persons from countries with less-developed systems of social protection might wish to move to countries with more-developed systems in order to avail of the more generous benefits in those countries – a phenomenon which has come to be termed 'social tourism'. This would particularly be the case where health care is of a higher standard and where there are relatively generous cash benefits available for the unemployed and families with children.

The EC Commission sought to draw attention to the common problems facing systems of social security and, in particular, the implications of the Single Market and greater economic integration for such systems and policies, through a series of studies and international seminars in the run up to 1992. The fruits of this first emerged at a meeting of the Council of Ministers for Social Security in September 1989 under the French Presidency. It was formally recognised that member states face common problems in the field of social protection and that the development of social protection systems was being influenced by the need to tackle these common problems.

Accordingly, the Council proposed that the '*de facto* convergence' which was occurring should be further formalised by establishing common objectives as a guide for national policies. A Resolution (non-binding) on combating social exclusion (OJ No. C277, 31.10.1989 p.1) was also adopted by the Council at that meeting in which the importance of ensuring complementarity between policies aimed at ensuring that all categories of the population have a guarantee of resources and of policies aimed at economic and social integration of disadvantaged social groups was emphasised.

The "Social Charter", and Action Programmes

The importance of the social dimension of greater European integration was recognised later in 1989 through the adoption by 11 member states (including Ireland, but excluding the UK) on 9 December, 1989, of the

European Social Charter. It is recognised in the Charter that completion of the Single Market should offer improvements in the social field for workers, especially in terms of social protection, and above all, that retrogression must be avoided. Paragraph 10 of the Charter provides that workers must have a right to adequate social protection and an adequate level of social security benefits. Those unable to enter or re-enter the labour market, and who have no means of subsistence would be able to receive sufficient resources and social assistance in keeping with their particular situation. Similar provision is made in paragraphs 24 and 25 of the Charter in the case of workers who are retired and in the case of those who when they retire are not entitled to a pension.

The Commission of the EC published an *Action Programme* to accompany the Social Charter and explain how it would be implemented [Com (89) 568]. The Commission noted that differences in social security cover might act as a serious brake on the free movement of workers and exacerbate regional imbalances, particularly, between the North and South of the Community. Accordingly, following on from the proposal of the Council of Ministers for Social Security the previous September, they indicated that they would bring forward proposals for *Council Recommendations* as distinct from Directives on:

the *convergence of social protection* objectives and policies,

and on

common criteria concerning *sufficient resources and social assistance* in the social protection systems (commonly referred to as "minimum income" or "minimum resources").

An *ad hoc* group of senior officials representing the member states was set up to advise the Commission on the drawing up of the draft texts for the Recommendations, under the aegis of the Group of Directors General for Social Security. Advice was also obtained from a group of academic experts and the social partners – employers and trade unions – were consulted through their organisations at EC level. International seminars on the subjects took place. An informal Council of Ministers for Social Security was organised by the Irish Presidency on 27 April, 1990 to afford Ministers an opportunity to have an in-depth discussion on convergence. It was also designed to assist the Commission in coming up with proposals that were likely to be acceptable to member states. It emerged from the discussions that there was a general consensus in favour of the process being undertaken by the Commission and clear guidelines were provided for drawing up the texts of the proposed Recommendations.

What Convergence Means

The Recommendation on convergence of Social Protection Systems, submitted to the Council of Ministers in June 1991 and adopted in July 1992, sets out in broad terms the objectives for social protection shared by all the member states (OJ No. L245 of 26.8.92 p. 49).

Responsibility for meeting these objectives in terms of organisation, delivery of services, award and payment of cash benefits and ways of financing the system, remains at national level and in this regard the recommendation is very much in line with the principle of subsidiarity, which was reinforced in the Treaty of Maastricht.

Progress in meeting the objectives laid down will be monitored by the EC Commission. This will involve an analysis and evaluation of the effectiveness of the various policies being pursued in the different member states in terms of the outcomes being achieved for the resources used. A regular report on social protection in the EC will be prepared, outlining and evaluating the progress being achieved by each member state in meeting the common objectives. The EC Commission will also be required to organise regular consultations with the member states on the development of social protection policy. A mutual information system on social protection (MISSOC) which provides for the exchange of information on all social protection developments in the various member states has been set up and should greatly facilitate the process.

The following have been identified in the Recommendation as the main tasks of systems of social protection:

- to guarantee all residents in a State a level of resources in keeping with human dignity (the subject of the separate Recommendation on the Guarantee of Minimum Resources – see below) and access to essential health services regardless of income

- to contribute to the social integration of all residents and the economic integration of those who are in a position to exercise a gainful activity

- to provide employed workers with a replacement income which will maintain their standard of living in a reasonable manner, in the event of illness, accident, maternity, invalidity, unemployment or retirement
- to examine the possibility of introducing and/or developing appropriate social protection for self-employed persons.

Benefits under the systems should be granted in accordance with the following principles:

- equal treatment, so as to avoid any discrimination based on nationality, race, gender, religion, customs or political opinion
- fairness, so that those dependent on social protection receive their fair share from improvements in the standard of living of the population as a whole, while taking account of priorities at national level.

It is also recommended that social protection systems, while adhering to the above principles, must endeavour to adapt to the social and economic changes, in particular, those which effect family structures and the labour market, as well as to demographic changes. In the context of the tasks and principles set down and the need for the systems to adapt to economic and social changes, general objectives are proposed for each main area – sickness, maternity, unemployment, the elderly and the family.

Guarantee of Minimum Resources

On 13 May 1991, the Commission submitted its proposal for a recommendation on common criteria concerning resources and social assistance in the social protection systems which was adopted on 24 June 1992 (OJ No. L245 of 26.8.92 p. 46). The aim of the recommendation is to define the common principles according to which a general right to sufficient resources and benefits should be guaranteed within the social protection systems of each member state.

Accordingly, it:

- recommends that Member States recognise the basic right of a person to sufficient resources and social assistance to live in a manner compatible with human dignity as part of a comprehensive and consistent drive to combat social exclusion

- lays down general principles on how the gaps in existing systems of social protection should be adapted to guarantee to the persons concerned a minimum of sufficient stable and regular resources and to encourage their access to the rights, benefits and services contributing to economic and social integration
- sets out methods of implementation in relation to the calculation and regular adjustment of the aid to be given and supporting resources
- invites the Member States to make the provisions necessary for the progressive implementation of this right and for the assessment of the progress being made in this regard on an ongoing basis.

As in the case of convergence, the Recommendation also envisages the EC Commission encouraging and organising the systematic exchange of information and experiences, and the continued evaluation of the provisions adopted, and reporting on the progress achieved and the obstacles encountered during implementation.

Extension of EC Competence

In contrast with the case of the Social Charter and the Agreement on Social Policy in the Treaty on European Union, the Recommendations providing for the new strategy on social protection have been adopted by the 12 member states, including the United Kingdom, and represent a significant, if modest, extension of EC competence in this area.

The need for further initiatives is likely to emerge from monitoring the progress being achieved in meeting the objectives laid down. If action at Community level is necessary to maintain progress in this regard or to avoid retrogression, there is now a basis for doing so in the Agreement on Social Policy attached to the Treaty of Maastricht.

The Role of the Commission Monitoring the progress being made towards achieving the objectives set down in the Recommendations, and generally in relation to the further development of proper social protection, will be of crucial importance in the whole process. It will be necessary for the Commission to devise a system for clearly and accurately measuring the development of systems of social protection in the various member states. This should involve, in effect, the Commission holding up a mirror to individual states and to the European Community as a whole, which will clearly reflect the progress being made in achieving the objectives laid down.

The process should bring home to individual member states the areas in which the least progress is being made and the categories of those in need of social protection who are faring the worst. This may give rise to the necessary political pressure at national level to remedy the situation. The process should also facilitate assessments of the effectiveness of the various national systems of social protection. The diversity of such systems among the member states can be a real advantage in this regard, as it results in different approaches being taken to similar problems which can be evaluated on an ongoing basis as to their effectiveness and comparisons made.

In the context of the Single Market and given the major problems which systems of social protection in all member states will have to cope with, it is essential that they operate as cost effectively as possible. Priority, therefore, will have to be given in developing ways of comparing outcomes in the various fields of social protection among member states for the level of resources being used. If through this process it is established that a relatively poor return is being achieved in any area for the level of resources being used, this will in itself provide a major impetus to change to a more effective system.

A further broad issue which will have to be addressed on an ongoing basis concerns the extent to which the correct balance is being maintained between the development of the conditions necessary to facilitate and promote economic development and making sufficient resources available to continually and steadily improve systems of social protection. It goes without saying that it is necessary to generate wealth and to create jobs through economic development if the necessary resources are to be available to improve systems of social protection. Measures, however desirable, which undermine the capacity of a member state to achieve such development on a continuing basis would also undermine the capacity to improve its systems of social protection in the longer term. It is also essential to avoid being over cautious regarding the development of systems of social protection in order to achieve economic development. It has to be recognised that those in need of social protection should not be left to wait any longer than is absolutely necessary for the extra resources needed to improve the quality of their lives. Inadequate social protection causes real suffering and hardship to many people. The positive contribution which social protection can make in supporting economic activity must also be recognised, particularly in terms of a healthy, trained and committed workforce and the impact on purchasing power effected by the redistribution of income.

The primary aim, therefore, should be to obtain the right mix of policies to maximise the level and quality of the social protection provided in a way that is economically sustainable. Again, it should be possible to obtain clear indications of what the right mix of policies is in this regard by making comparisons between the various member states, allowing at the same time for the differing levels of economic development.

Role of the Member States The main responsibility for achieving the objectives laid down is left to member states. Given greater economic integration in the context of the Single Market and Economic and Monetary Union, member states will have to operate within similar limits in terms of the resources they can devote to social protection. At the same time they will all have to tackle similar problems in the field of social protection, resulting from social, economic and the demographic changes which are, and have been, taking place. In the light of this reality, it is expected that systems of social protection will evolve on converging lines as member states seek to meet the common objectives laid down in the recommendations in a way that will enable them to maintain economic competitiveness with the European Community.

We now go on to give a brief overview of the main issues member states will face in this regard in the years ahead.

SOCIAL PROTECTION: THE CURRENT ISSUES

Financing Social Protection

The main issue that all member states are now facing is how best can provision be made for the financing of the growing burden of social protection. The main source of finance in the majority of member states has been social insurance contributions, deducted directly from the wages/salaries of employees and from the self-employed. The relatively high and persistent level of unemployment and unstable employment has reduced significantly the potential in real terms of this method of financing social protection. Not only is revenue curtailed, if there are fewer contributors, but high levels of contributions can have a negative impact on employment creation by increasing the cost of employing people. Accordingly, this method of financing social protection may have to be scaled back in real terms by all member states in the years ahead.

There are two other main sources of finance for social protection – *general taxation* and voluntary provision through *occupational schemes*.

General Taxation This may be used more as a source of finance for benefits such as health care and family benefits, which are not directly related to employment. Social insurance contributions, therefore, are likely to be confined to financing cash benefits for contingencies related to work, for example incapacity for work, and retirement. The conditions for entitlement to cash benefits under social insurance may be tightened, which will result in more people failing to qualify for social insurance benefits and having to rely on social assistance, which is normally financed by general taxation. Governments may also restrict increases in the rates of contribution, by providing subventions to social insurance from taxation to meet the resulting shortfall in income. Relief from contributions may also be provided for in the case of employees on low earnings as a way of reducing disincentives to the creation and take up of such employment. The types of measure outlined above would result in a new distribution, as between taxation and social insurance contributions, of financing for social protection.

Occupational Schemes The level and range of benefits provided under systems of social insurance can also be curtailed by reducing the replacement rate which cash benefits and pensions provide for those on higher earnings. This would result in an increasing role for *occupational schemes* which provide supplementary cover, for short-term benefits, such as sick pay, permanent health insurance (in the case of long-term incapacity for work), retirement pensions and death benefits for surviving dependants. These occupational schemes are normally established through collective bargaining on an industry/

service-wide level or at company level. Individuals on higher earnings, in particular the self-employed, can also purchase extra cover from private insurance companies. Insurance cover for health care is also being increasingly availed of by persons on higher incomes, being purchased either by individuals or by companies on behalf of their employees. Occupational and private insurance cover can be promoted by the state through allowing for tax relief on the contributions made.

"Pay-as-you-go" and Funding

In addition to the perceived need to reduce, or at least avoid increasing, rates of social insurance contributions in the interests of employment creation, there is also a need for measures to reduce the burden on the next generation of financing pensions, health and welfare services for an ageing population. The ageing of the population has given rise to potentially serious problems for *'pay-as-you-go' systems* under which pensions and other services are financed from current revenue. The proportion of contributors to pensioners in EC member states is set to decline from 5:1, which has been the position in recent decades, to less than 3:1 in the early decades of the next century. This means that the burden on contributors of financing pensions will be much greater than it is at present. This will be added to further by the increased costs of providing for the growing numbers of very elderly people, who will require more health care, given the higher incidence of infirmity with increasing age, and more welfare and support services, since family members are unlikely to be available to the same extent as in the past to provide care and support on an unpaid basis.

Funding This involves the setting aside of resources to finance the provision of benefits in the future. It can facilitate spreading the costs of financing benefits more evenly and reducing the net cost by exploiting investment opportunities. Funding as a method of financing social protection is normally used to finance second tier income-related pensions under occupational schemes and additional third tier personal pensions. It may also come to be used more widely to finance the provision of welfare and support services for the frail elderly.

It is argued that funding may not, in fact, reduce the burden on the next generation of providing for the increasing proportion of elderly in the population, as the resources required will still have to come from the wealth generated by the economically active at that time, the only difference being that funding results in the resources coming from investment returns, as opposed to contributions and taxes levied directly on incomes under a 'pay-as-you-go' system (Communication of EC Commission on occupational pension schemes). Part of the resources set aside under the funding method can, however, be invested in other countries which enables social protection to be financed from the wealth created by the economically active in those countries, as well as one's own. It is also the case that it is easier to draw down income from returns on investment than from direct contributions and taxes, particularly if these are already at a high level.

Another consideration is that the methods adopted for financing pensions can have important macroeconomic effects. Funding can result in significant resources being accumulated for long term investment, of which there is a shortage world wide at present, while the 'pay-as-you-go' systems support aggregate demand in the economy. Over-reliance on either method of financing pensions can have negative economic consequences both for individual countries and the EC generally. Accordingly, this is another dimension of policy on social protection which will need to be closely monitored both at national and EC levels(see also section on Employment Creation P.104).

The Role of the State

Social Protection: Public v Private Provision The growth in occupational and private provision of social protection cover in relation to cash benefits and health and welfare services may be paralleled by a growth in the provision of social protection services by service providers in the private sector. Systems of social provision in the widest sense, including education, training, health care, income maintenance services, absorb a high proportion of a country's resources and are a major source of employment in each state. However, these services which are directly provided by the state are not subject to the 'disciplines of the market' in the same way as services provided in the private sector. It can be difficult, therefore, to compare public and private service providers on the grounds of efficiency and cost effectiveness.

A distinction may increasingly be drawn between, on the one hand, the state providing services directly and, on the other hand, the state purchasing services of this nature, which are not provided by its own employees. Where the state purchases services this allows for competition between service providers which may promote greater efficiency and cost effectiveness. The areas where there may be most scope for this approach would be in services relating to the provision of health care, the care of the elderly and incapacitated, education and employment training.

Integration of the Marginalised There is real concern that if systems of social protection evolve in the ways outlined above, a two-tier system will emerge with one level of cover for those in stable and well-paid employment and a significantly inferior level for those categories of the population who are in low-paid, unstable employment, unemployed, or effectively excluded from employment because of family responsibilities, incapacity for work or age. Accordingly, another major issue facing member states is how to provide for the social and, where appropriate, economic integration of these groups who otherwise may be excluded from the mainstream of society as a result of the social, economic and demographic changes taking place.

Income adequacy, which is one of the main ways of achieving 'integration', can generally only be obtained through regular employment. Employment also helps to integrate people into society by providing a sense of dignity and worth and a socially-acceptable structure to their lives in terms of activity, social contacts with fellow workers, work-related pastimes and leisure activities. It is essential, therefore, that persons who are unemployed are given the necessary training, work experience and assistance with job search and placement to enable them to obtain employment. Special measures are also needed to enable persons with family responsibilities, in particular, those in the younger age groups, to combine those responsibilities with employment, initially, perhaps, on a part-time basis leading eventually to full-time employment. These may include family income support to supplement earnings and Community services to provide day care for children and for incapacitated and elderly relatives. Rehabilitation services for persons suffering from physical or mental incapacity are also required to enable such persons obtain employment.

Employment Creation This also has to be promoted. It may require curtailing, at least in real terms, the level of taxation and contributions payable by employees in order to reduce the cost of employing people. Consideration may have to be given in this regard to restructuring social insurance contributions by raising or eliminating income ceilings on contributions, which mainly benefit the higher paid, in favour of reducing the rate of contribution payable by the lower paid. It is the case that many jobs may not provide an adequate income, particularly for persons with family responsibilities. It may be necessary, therefore, in the interests of promoting economic integration for systems of social protection to provide regular income support to persons in low-wage employment.

It also has to be borne in mind in this context that a major source of employment is, and will continue to be, the 'Welfare State' itself. The state uses a high proportion of the income obtained from tax and social security contributions to finance the direct provision or the purchase of services such as education, training, health, welfare, income maintenance, which provide employment for the most part within the state. The redistribution of wealth effected through systems of social protection involves the redistribution of purchasing power.

Social security systems redistribute income to the unemployed, the incapacitated, and the elderly who in general spend a higher proportion of their income on home produced goods and services than would be the case with economically active persons, particularly those who are more highly paid. The state also influences purchasing power through the use of tax reliefs. Tax reliefs, for example, on mortgages and contributions to health insurance, influence the extent to which taxpayers spend their income on housing and private health care, both of which create employment within the state. The state can also encourage saving for investment, most notably through deferring tax on income set aside for occupational pensions, until such time as the pensions are paid.

Social Integration Economic integration through the provision of a basic income and regular employment is, as pointed out above, one of the most important means of achieving social integration, in particular, for those in the economically active age groups. However, there is also a need for additional measures for those who cannot obtain employment, for example, because of family responsibilities – care of young children, incapacitated and/or elderly relatives – and for those who are themselves incapacitated or retired from employment. Community services are required to provide support for the persons concerned and to facilitate their participation in social life. Of particular importance in this regard are personal development courses and programmes, which not only provide a regular social outlet but also promote initiative and greater self-sufficiency, thus counteracting the dependency that systems of social protection can create.

The social integration of the growing proportion of elderly people in the population will be one of the major challenges in the decades ahead. Increasing numbers are now retired at the age of 60 from their main employment and many can look forward to periods of retirement of 20 years and over. For at least the first half of that period, the persons concerned can make an active contribution to society through temporary and part-time employment, providing support for younger members of their families, and engaging in voluntary community and social activities. They, in turn, will require support from family and community services, if they are to remain living in their own homes and retain an involvement with the local community, as they become more infirm.

1993 has been designated by the EC as "The European Year of Older People and Solidarity between the Generations" and this should serve to focus attention on the problems and opportunities presented by the growing numbers of elderly people in the population.

We have examined in general terms the policy which has been developed at EC level to promote a Community-wide approach to resolving the common problems each member state faces in the field of social protection but which at the same time, in line with the principle of subsidiarity, leaves responsibility largely at national level for adopting and developing systems of social protection to cope with these problems. The next chapter contains a brief analysis of how the system of social protection in Ireland is being developed in this regard.

8. SOCIAL PROTECTION IN IRELAND

Gerry Mangan

What are the likely implications for Ireland of the EC moves towards convergence of social protection? Any views of what the future holds, as seen from mid -1993, must be highly speculative. This chapter presents one particular view. It begins with a description of the present social protection system in Ireland and an explanation of how it has evolved in recent decades. The Irish system is then related to the issues, already discussed in Chapter 7, which have arisen at EC level.

THE IRISH SOCIAL PROTECTION SYSTEM

The Context of the System

The Demographic Context Ireland is experiencing similar problems to those facing other EC member states (see Chapter 3), but in most respects they are more acute. Ireland has by far the highest age dependency ratio in the EC (108.7), as compared to an average of 82.4 for the EC as a whole, as the table below shows for 1990. This is mainly due to the high proportion of the population aged under 20, since Ireland has the lowest proportion aged 60 and over.

Economic and Social Context This high dependency ratio is compounded by the fact that we have one of the highest levels of18% (almost twice the EC average), the lowest female participation rate in the workforce at 32% (see Chapter 2) and, in line with similar trends in other EC countries, increasing numbers of lone-parent families.

TABLE 6

Demographic Situation in EC Countries, 1990

Country	Total Population (000s)	% aged 0-19	% aged 20-59	% aged 60+	Age Dependency Ratio*
Belgium	9,948	24.8	54.7	20.4	82.7
Denmark	5,135	24.3	55.3	20.4	80.8
Germany	79,113	21.8	57.9	20.3	72.8
Greece	10,204	26.8	53.8	19.4	85.7
Spain	38,924	28.5	53.0	18.5	88.7
France	56,581	27.8	53.2	19.0	88.0
Ireland	3,508	36.9	47.9	15.1	108.7
Italy	57,576	24.4	55.4	20.2	80.5
Luxembourg	378	23.2	57.9	18.9	72.8
Netherlands	14,893	25.7	57.0	17.3	75.3
Portugal	10,337	29.3	52.5	18.2	90.5
UK.	57,313	25.9	53.3	20.7	87.4
Eur 12	343,911	25.5	54.8	19.7	82.4

*Population aged 0-19 and 60+ relative to population aged 20-59.
Source: Courtney – derived from Tables 9, 12, 14, 17, 19.

In addition, Ireland is among those countries in the EC with a high level of public sector debt as a proportion of GDP – currently over 100%. In the context of Economic and Monetary Union, this has to be brought down to at most 60% of GDP before the end of the decade. We also have one of the most open economies in the EC. In 1988, exports represented the equivalent in value of 57.2% of GDP and imports, 47.5% of GDP (OECD). This means that the maintenance of economic competitiveness is essential if we are to create employment and generate the wealth necessary to provide for an adequate system of social protection for our high dependent population.

Type of System

Ireland has largely adopted the European Social Model in relation to social protection. In 1989, 20.6% of GDP was devoted to social protection which was ahead of Greece, Spain and Portugal and very close to the United Kingdom (see Chapter 3).

However, it has to be borne in mind in this regard that Ireland has a significantly higher dependency ratio and a higher level of unemployment than those countries. Therefore, the resources for social protection have to be spread more thinly. Also GDP per capita in Ireland in 1990 was just 69% of the EC average (see Chapter 2).

The development of the Irish social protection system began when Ireland was still fully part of the United Kingdom. It has continued to be very much influenced by developments in the UK, as demonstrated by the adoption of the Beveridge model in the post-war period, implicitly if not explicitly. An outline of the respective roles currently of social insurance, schemes financed from general taxation and occupational/private insurance schemes in the provision of social protection follows.

Social Insurance Social insurance contributions finance flat-rate short-term benefits for disability, maternity, occupational injuries and diseases and unemployment, and flat-rate pensions for invalidity, widows and orphans, deserted wives, retirement/old age. Virtually all income earners between the ages 16 and 66 are compulsorily insured, but cover for the self-employed is limited to widow's and orphan's and old age pensions. Certain public servants have limited social insurance cover only, on the grounds that they have state-backed occupational cover as part of their terms of employment.

In the 1970s, after entry to the EC, Ireland appeared to be set to develop significantly the social insurance system by introducing pay-related social insurance contributions (PRSI) and extending cover to provide second-tier *earnings related* benefits and pensions. (The flat-rate benefits and pensions comprise what is usually called the first tier). However, as a result mainly of the serious economic difficulties experienced in the 1980s, and in particular the steep rise in unemployment, this did not happen. The pay-related benefits payable with short-term benefits introduced at that time have since been reduced and in the case of disability benefit phased out, and the option of an income-related pension scheme, set out in a Green Paper published in 1976, has not been proceeded with. However, the pay-related contributions introduced in 1979 which now finance mainly flat-rate benefits, have been retained.

In the period since 1980, resources have been concentrated on increasing the basic levels of payments to bring them up from a relatively low base to minimally adequate levels, and in extending basic social insurance cover to categories hitherto excluded, the self-employed in 1988 and those in part-time employment in 1990. The increase in payments over that period were 16% for short-term benefits and 22% for pensions, as compared to a real increase of just 14% in the average industrial wage over the same period. This overall approach was in line with the proposals of the Commission on Social Welfare, set up by the government to review the system, which reported in 1986.

Conditions for entitlement to benefits under social insurance have been tightened in recent years. The number of contributions required to qualify for certain benefits has been increased which has the effect of restricting entitlement to those in regular employment for longer periods. Income tests have been introduced to determine dependency, in the case of allowances for adult dependants (payable with weekly social insurance benefits) and for benefits for deserted wives. Entitlement to dental and optical benefits under the social insurance system has been restricted to those whose annual earnings are below a specified limit.

Reductions in real terms in social insurance expenditure achieved by these restrictions are justified as avoiding increases in the percentage rate of PRSI contributions, which add to the cost of employing people, particularly in relatively low-wage employments. Given the high level of unemployment in Ireland, further changes to social insurance schemes on these lines could be on the policy agenda in the years ahead.

Schemes Financed From General Taxation Ireland has a well developed system of social assistance financed from general taxation which provides basic income guarantees to all residents. Special social assistance schemes provide weekly benefits, which are subject to a means test, to the elderly , the widowed, lone parents (including the widowed), those caring for incapacitated relatives, those permanently incapable of work and the unemployed. There is also a pre-retirement allowance scheme for those aged 55 or over who have been unemployed for at least 15 months and who consider themselves retired from the labour force. A Supplementary Welfare Allowance scheme provides payments to those with insufficient incomes who do not qualify under the special schemes or who need assistance with exceptional needs. A family income supplement scheme provides income support for families with children, where at least one of the parents is in employment. Monthly child benefit is payable to all families with children up to age 16 (18, if school going) without a means test.

Increases in social assistance payments of a similar scale in real terms to those provided for under social insurance were also made in the period since 1980.

Schemes of social assistance are likely to continue to have a significant role for the foreseeable future in providing social protection for those who are unable to obtain cover under social insurance and occupational schemes, which is dependent on having regular employment. They may also come to have an increasing role in reducing the cost of employing people by providing income support for employees on low wages, in particular, for those with child dependants.

The state health services in Ireland are financed mainly from general taxation (81.5%). A special health contribution levied on all income (1.25%, up to an income ceiling) finances 8.9% of expenditure and the remainder (9.6% approximately), is financed from direct public hospital earnings from semi-private and private beds (Ryan, 1992).

Those in the lower income groups, which comprise approximately 38% of the population, are eligible for the full range of health care services without charge. The remainder of the population are eligible for full in-hospital care in public wards, subject to a nominal charge. They must, however, pay for non-hospital primary care, except that some financial assistance towards the cost of drugs and medicines and for dental and optical treatment for children is available.

There is unlikely to be any significant change in the foreseeable future in the structures for financing the state health services. The main emphasis is likely to be on containing the cost of providing these services, through the more efficient use of resources and an increasing emphasis on community-based services with a corresponding reduction in institutionalised care.

Occupational / Private Insurance Schemes As a result of the limited cover provided under the state system of social protection, persons on higher incomes have come to rely to a significant degree on occupational and private insurance schemes to provide supplementary cover. The Voluntary Health Insurance Board provides private health cover for 1.29 million members. A further 50,000 persons are insured for health care by a variety of small occupational or industry-based schemes. Tax relief is available for contributions to these schemes. It is estimated that in 1992 expenditure on health care services by these schemes will amount to £180 million or 9% of total expenditure on health care (Ryan, 1992).

Occupational schemes financed on a 'pay-as-you-go' basis provide cover for salary-related pensions and benefits for up to 200,000 employees in the public service (14% approx. of the labour force). Members of these schemes are exempt from full social insurance cover. A further 271,515 employees in the private sector and the commercial public sector are members of funded occupational pension schemes (20% approx. of the labour force). Many of those would also be eligible for 'sick pay' in the event of short-term sickness. It is estimated also that there may be up to 35,000 self-employed people with private insurance cover for pensions. In 1975, the total assets of funded occupational pension schemes amounted to IR£210 million, equivalent to 5.5% of GNP (Hughes). By 1991, the assets had grown to £9.3 billion, equivalent to 38% of GNP (IAPF – 1991). It is also estimated that in 1991 the net new cashflow into the pension funds was IR£333 million (IAPF – 1991). Asset accumulation is, therefore, increasing at a significant rate, and this trend is likely to continue for some time as most funded schemes will not reach maturity until well into the next century.

The state in Ireland has sought to encourage and promote the development of occupational pension arrangements through deferring income tax on resources set aside for pension purposes. Accordingly, public servants in unfunded schemes are not taxed on the monetary value of the annual pension promise they earn. Similarly, tax is not levied on the resources being accumulated in funded schemes, by way of contributions and returns on investments, to pay pensions to persons covered by such type schemes in the private sector and the commercial semi-state sector.

More recently, the state has provided for the regulation of occupational pension schemes to safeguard pension rights by the enactment of the Pensions Act, 1990 which came into operation with effect from 1 January 1991. The Act sets down the basic duties of scheme trustees in relation to the administration of schemes, and requires the trustees to provide for the preservation of benefits for members who change jobs, comply with a funding standard, in the case of defined benefit schemes, disclose full information to members on their own individual entitlements and on the administration of the scheme, and in particular, its financial viability, and comply with the principle of equal treatment for men and women. Scheme members also have a right to participate in the selection of trustees. A Pensions Board comprising representatives of government, employers, trade unions, pension funds, life assurance companies and the actuarial, accounting and legal professions, has been set up under the Act to supervise its operation.

SOCIAL PROTECTION IN IRELAND IN A MORE INTEGRATED EC

The structure of the social protection system in Ireland has been determined as in other EC countries by our history and culture, the social, economic and demographic changes taking place and, with a small open economy, our need to maintain economic competitiveness.

The limited role which compulsory social insurance has in the overall system of social protection, relative to most other EC countries, has been greatly influenced by the need to keep down the cost of employing people, given our high rates of unemployment and emigration. As a result, schemes of social assistance and family income support financed from general taxation, form a significant part of the social protection system. This is also related to the fact that we currently have in Ireland the highest demographic dependency ratio in the EC. The structure and financing (mainly from taxation) of our health services have also been greatly influenced by these factors.

It is necessary at the same time to provide a satisfactory level of social protection for those on higher earnings. This is being achieved by the promotion of voluntary supplementary cover for benefits/ pensions and health services under occupational/private insurance schemes through the system of tax reliefs on contributions to such schemes and on investment returns. The funding method of financing occupational pension schemes in the private and commercial semi-state sectors should also serve to ease the burden on future generations of providing for an ageing population.

The overall structure of the social protection system in Ireland does not appear, therefore, to require fundamental changes in order to maintain economic competitiveness within a more integrated EC. In fact, the social protection systems in the other EC countries which are faced with similar problems to those of Ireland arising from the social, economic and demographic changes taking place, could converge towards the type of system which has been evolving in this country.

It will be a major advantage in the years ahead for policymakers in Ireland, and for the public generally, to have the effectiveness of the Irish system of social protection compared to those of other EC countries, in the context of the strategy for convergence, which is now coming into operation at EC level. Of particular importance in this regard will be the extent to which it is considered we can sustain the current overall level of social protection, given our stage of economic development, and whether it should be possible to provide for higher such levels in real terms.

Social Protection and Mobility EC provision for the protection of the social security rights of people who move to other member states will continue to be of major importance for Ireland, given that emigration is likely to continue to be a reality for the foreseeable future. The priorities in this area are likely to include better protection for the unemployed and provision for the sharing of the costs of unemployment payments between countries where workers had been last employed and their country of origin, if they should return there. Equality of opportunity to obtain employment among EC citizens would also be greatly enhanced if persons seeking work in other states were entitled to the basic level of benefit payable to the unemployed in those states, at least, for a clearly defined period. This could be financed in part from the EC Budget.

Consideration may also be given in this context to improving EC wide access to health services. This would involve, for instance, Community citizens in countries with less-developed systems of health care being able to obtain treatment for acute illnesses in countries with more-developed systems, where such treatment would be more readily available. Economies of scale could also derive from this approach. Again, the costs involved could be borne in part by the EC Budget.

Monetary union, if it is achieved, will eliminate the costs and inconvenience for those with entitlements to pensions from more than one member state, of receiving the payments in different currencies. It should also enable procedures to be introduced providing for one pension payment to be made by, say, the competent institution in the country of residence of the pensioner, which could include provision for reimbursement of the expenditure involved between institutions in the various member states.

Protection of social security rights under occupational schemes in the case of persons who move to take up employment in other member states will also be a priority in the coming years. However, it is important for Ireland that the same level of security for such rights provided for under the Pensions Act is also provided for in other member states. This would be particularly the case if any provision were to be made for cross border membership of occupational pension schemes. Otherwise companies could locate the main administration of their schemes in countries which have more limited protection for such rights, as a way of reducing the costs of complying with proper safeguards.

Minimum Standards in Social Protection If member states begin to resort to 'social devaluation' i.e. reducing expenditure in real terms and standards generally in relation to social protection to maintain economic competitiveness, consideration may have to be given to introducing binding EC Directives prescribing minimum standards.

However, the less-economically developed states, such as Ireland, may not find it possible to agree to be bound by standards, however desirable, adherence to which may not be economically sustainable for them. The alternatives in these instances would be derogations for these states for set periods, which would undermine the effect of prescribing standards, or direct Community assistance for prescribed transitional periods involving a transfer of resources until such time as they could sustain compliance with the standards from their own resources.

There is no provision made at present for the direct transfer of resources to the less-economically developed states to assist in financing their systems of social protection. The main financial support given is through the Structural Funds, including the Cohesion Fund agreed at Maastricht, which assist these states in developing their economic capacity. It is hoped that this will, in turn, facilitate the creation of more wealth to finance social protection.

The Social Fund is particularly relevant to social protection as it finances training and employment initiatives for the young and long-term unemployed which assists them in obtaining regular employment, thus reducing the burden on systems of social protection.

However, the question of going further than financial support through the Structural Funds to assist the less-developed states finance a level of social protection which meets basic EC-wide standards, will have to be considered in the years ahead. If it transpires that these states do not have the capacity to finance adequate levels of social protection and at the same time remain economically competitive, the issue of direct financial support being made available from the EC Budget in the interests of promoting economic and social cohesion will have to be faced.

Conclusion

The development of the social protection system in Ireland has been very much influenced by the need to maintain economic competitiveness and at the same time provide for a much higher proportion of the population dependent on social protection than is the case currently in any other EC member state. Despite the approach adopted, it will be very difficult for Ireland to create the wealth required in the foreseeable future to bring levels of social protection progressively closer to those which obtain in the more-developed EC member states.

EC policy on coordination of social security systems and on the transfer of resources to Ireland and the other less-developed states will have to reflect this reality, if significant progress towards social and economic cohesion within the EC is to be achieved.

9. IRELAND IN A EUROPEAN WELFARE STATE?

Séamus Ó Cinnéide

This last chapter begins with a summary account of the present state of social policy in Ireland, or the Welfare State to use the more evocative term. Where do we go from here with our Welfare State, and what difference could our membership of the EC make? We review the salient points from earlier chapters about EC membership and its impact to date in Ireland. We acknowledge that responsibility for our own social problems begins in Ireland: we must initiate the necessary process of reform ourselves. Lastly, we look to the future: how is the EC "social dimension" likely to develop and what should we in Ireland do about it?

In this volume, our purpose is to describe and analyse what social policy means in the EC context and how it relates to social policy in Ireland. As far as social policy in Ireland is concerned we revert to the conventional and comprehensive definition. Social policy encompasses all the social services and measures which are directly redistributive; this whole area corresponds to what is often called the Welfare State.[2]

Policy is never static: it is always changing, being modified, extended or, more rarely, contracted. In the perspective of this volume, policy analysis is not an end in itself: policy is something to be shaped and not just to be studied. In its comprehensive review of Ireland's performance in, and gains from, the EC, the National Economic and Social Council emphasised that the social dimension is of extreme importance. It is inextricably linked with the process of economic

---

2. In recent years the term "social policy" has been used by some commentators to refer to policies relating to such issues as divorce and abortion, which is quite a different usage from that adopted here.

integration and "cannot be seen simply as a separate set of regulations or expenditure programmes"; it is especially significant for less developed economies such as that of Ireland; its development would contribute to the stability and cohesion of the Community as a whole. "An integrated European economy with a unified labour market and a common currency may also inescapably require some integration of the Community's Welfare States" (NESC, 1989, pp. 513, 555).

More to the point,

> Ireland must contribute positively to formulating the agenda for the Community's social policy discussions. This is necessary because Ireland, and other peripheral economies, may have different social policy preoccupations to the wealthier central economies (*ibid.*, p. 554).

What should Ireland be saying or doing? We cannot provide the answers here but we can, and will, make a start in four ways:

- firstly, by taking stock of the Irish Welfare State
- secondly, by drawing out some of the conclusions from previous chapters
- thirdly, by considering what we need to do in Ireland in relation to social policy
- fourthly, by exploring the possibilities of development of social policy in the EC.

THE IRISH WELFARE STATE

It is now fifty years since the Beveridge Report in Britain which gave rise to the extensive post-war social policy innovations in that country which, taken together, comprised and became known as the Welfare State. Beveridge was widely discussed in Ireland. It hastened the introduction of Children's Allowances in 1944 and the establishment of the Department of Social Welfare in 1948. For a long time, social policy developments in Ireland lagged far behind those in Britain, but from the 1960s the pace of development of social policy in Ireland accelerated considerably. In the past three decades we have constructed our own Welfare State which now rivals that of our neighbour (see

Social Security Benefits, Northern Ireland & Republic of Ireland, 1990, for example) and exceeds what our performance might be expected to be, given our level of economic development and our peripherality.

This is easy to illustrate, but difficult to prove. There are problems of definition and problems of comparison. In Britain, the Welfare State is usually taken to mean the totality of social services and direct redistributive measures. In the Nordic countries, they also include market regulatory measures which *indirectly* affect the distribution of incomes, resources and life chances. Ringen (1987) elaborates this distinction between redistributive policies and regulatory policies but it suits us here, like Ringen, to concentrate on redistributive policies only.

However, the most recent analysts of the Irish Welfare State, O'Connell and Rottman, choose the wider definition, involving, in fact, a three-fold division:

- policies directed at the number and structure of positions in the labour market, i.e. job creation
- policies on equality of opportunity, especially education policy and policy on men/women equality in the labour force
- taxes and direct benefits, including social welfare, health services, education and housing (1992, pp. 210, 211).

These authors describe in some detail the expansion of the Welfare State in Ireland over the past three decades. For them, the key concept is social citizenship "the bundle of social rights – to welfare, equality and security – to which citizens are entitled, unconditionally, by virtue of their membership of the national community"; these rights have expanded steadily over the years.

In a country overshadowed by Britain in relation to social policy as in other ways, it is necessary to spell out the extensiveness of our own Welfare State (Coughlan, 1984). The Welfare State is no mere appendage of government: the state in Ireland, as in many developed countries, is to a large extent a Welfare State. In 1992, nearly £7,000 million was spent on income transfers and social services (health services, education and housing); this represented 56% of all central government current expenditure, or 70% of expenditure excluding the servicing of the public debt. In Chapter 3, Gerry Mangan has presented

EUROSTAT figures which show that the percentage of GDP devoted to social protection in Ireland in 1989, 20.6%, is higher than it is in three other EC member states and does not fall far short of what it is in Italy and the UK, which are more prosperous countries. According to OECD figures, Ireland's expenditure on health care in 1987 represented a higher percentage of GDP, 6.9%, than in any other OECD country (Commission on Health Funding 1989, p.49). (Such figures are indicative of comparative magnitudes only and cannot be regarded as accurate measures of the level of development of services or of the extent to which needs are met).

In the cases of education and housing, we have comparative figures which could be regarded as measures of output rather than input. In 1986-87, the percentage of the age-group 15-19 in *full-time* education was 61% in Ireland as compared to 33% in Germany, 42% in the UK, 58% in Greece, 68% in France and 74% in Belgium (OECD, 1989). At 81%, Ireland has the highest proportion of housing units owner-occupied of any EC country, but a greater proportion of the rented sector is publicly owned (as distinct from privately owned or owned by housing associations) than in the other countries [Commission of the European Communities (CEC), 1992b].

One could go further, as O'Connell and Rottman have done, in relation to their wider definition of Welfare State, to highlight the pervasive intervention of the state in determining life chances and labour policies. However, it is sufficient for our purpose to indicate that Ireland's perspective on EC social policy must be that of a country with a highly-developed set of welfare state provisions and the problems or challenges that go with that. It is also salient that these provisions are supported by a public consensus which is reflected by the political parties. In 1975, Donnison found that the theme of "how to create a fairer and more equal society" . . . and the closely related one of expanding the Governments social expenditures, have been stressed in Ireland recently by all the main political parties, the Irish Congress of Trade Unions, voluntary bodies, Church authorities and the country's economic planners" (NESC, 1975, p. 49). A commentator on the situation ten years later could state that "the Irish political parties have shared a general consensus in favour of higher public spending, while at the same time they support the 'mixed' economy and reliance on private capital as the main motor of economic development". Social policy differences rarely influence elections. "No Irish party has gone before the electorate waving a monetarist banner and pledged to cut spending on Social Services" (Coughlan, 1984). This view is still valid despite the emergence in the intervening years of policy proposals that are usually identified with the New Right. One could add that the experience of the 1992 general election would suggest that welfare cuts are still unpopular with voters. The consensus in favour of the welfare state has also found expression to a greater or lesser extent in a series of corporatist "national agreements" between the Government, trade unions and employers. (Farming organisations are also involved, but in a more limited way). The latest of these agreements is the Programme for Economic and Social Progress (PESP) agreed and published in January 1991. The key objectives of this long-term strategy for "economic and social progress" are set out at the beginning. They consist of major economic objectives but also include:

- a major assault on long-term unemployment
- the development of greater social rights within our health, education, social welfare and housing services.

Section IV of the PESP, which deals with *Social Reform* or social policy, sets out policy proposals and commitments for, as it puts it, "major structural reform in particular in achieving greater social equity" (PESP, 1991). Section IV does not represent an integrated government strategy: it consists of a very limited number of fundamental initiatives and a diverse collection of policy proposals garnered from the various government departments, but also seeming to represent considerable trade union influence. However, it symbolises a commitment, and the consensus referred to above, and a point from which the debate on the future of the Welfare State in Ireland must go forward.

We will be resuming that debate here in the context of EC social policy. But if we want to know how developments in Ireland will be influenced by the EC, we need to review our experience of the EC so far.

THE INFLUENCE OF THE EC TO DATE

To what extent, and in what ways has Ireland's membership of the EC over the past twenty years influenced the development of the Welfare State in Ireland?

The evidence has been presented in earlier chapters, which have dealt with the different aspects of EC influence or impact. In Chapter 2, Larry Bond analysed the implications of EC membership for overall economic development, for employment and unemployment and for income distribution and poverty. In Chapter 4, and at the beginning of Chapter 7, Gerry Mangan described the main EC developments in relation to social protection: the measures to facilitate transferability of entitlement to benefits between countries ("measures to protect the social security entitlements of persons moving within the Community", to use the official terminology), and to promote equality between men and women, and the discussion on the harmonisation of social protection. In Chapter 5, Ita Mangan dealt with EC influences in Ireland under four headings: the European Social Fund; men/women equality; workers rights; and the smaller, but still influential, programmes dealing with deprived minorities. We can summarise this evidence by relating it to two aspects of the Welfare State: (a) the extent of needs to be met by the state and (b) the extent of resources available to meet those needs.

But first it must be acknowledged that apart from influences associated with the EC other factors have influenced, and will continue to influence, social policy not just in Ireland but in other comparable countries as well. Some of these have been dealt with by Gerry Mangan in Chapter 3, where he refers to social, demographic and economic change. Changing patterns of household formation, marriage and separation and divorce mean that many more one-parent families, headed by women outside the labour force, will need income support. Demographic change, especially the ageing of the population, will have implications for pensions and for health and welfare services, although in Ireland the worst effects of this trend will be delayed for longer than in any other EC country. The major increase in the younger age groups in Ireland over the past twenty five years has been contrary to EC trends and has, of course, had serious implications for education and for employment and unemployment.

The Extent of Needs to be Met

Membership of the EC could in principle have affected the extent of needs to be met within Ireland in three ways:

- in so far as it has led to more, or greater, poverty or other social problems

- to the extent that it has imposed greater social policy obligations on the state
- to the extent that it has given rise to greater expectations which are translated into higher demands.

Poverty Larry Bond has shown that in the past twenty years the distribution of income in Ireland has worsened. In 1973, 18% of the population had an income of less than half the average disposable income: in 1987, the figure was 23%. The families involved accounted for 16% of all children under 14 in 1973 and for 26% of all children in 1987. In that period, 1973-1987, incomes in general, including the lowest incomes, increased in real terms in Ireland and in other European countries. If poverty were measured in absolute terms, then there would be no poverty now as compared with twenty years ago or fifty years ago. It is widely accepted that poverty is relative to standards of living generally. It is from that point of view that things have disimproved. The increase in the incidence of poverty, to use the usual shorthand expression, was associated mainly with the increase in unemployment. Ireland's present unemployment rate is among the highest of all member states at almost twice the EC average, and four times what it was in 1973.

It is impossible of course to attribute this grim decline to EC membership: no one is prepared to say for sure, but the NESC cautiously suggests that "part of the rise in unemployment since accession is attributable . . . to the trade effects of EC membership" (NESC, 1989, p.515). On the other hand, Ireland must take responsibility for its own domestic policies. "The developmental policies pursued by Irish governments did not sufficiently, consistently or systematically address some key structural constraints on Irish economic development" and "priority was given to *short-term* goals by both government and society" (*ibid.*, p. 526).

Social Policy Obligations Membership of the EC has also put additional pressure on the Irish Welfare State in that Ireland has had to implement legislation, with costs attached to it, adopted by the Community. In some cases the costs fall on employers, for instance, in relation to the workers' rights provisions dealt with by Ita Mangan in Chapter 5. The additional costs to employers in implementing these highly desirable policy changes may in some cases have had the effect of making them reduce their work force, thus adding to the numbers of the unemployed more or less dependent on the state. In other cases, the costs have fallen on the state: the implementation of the EC Directive on equal treatment of men and women in social security matters (Council Directive 79/7/EEC) is a case in point. The Irish authorities were inordinately slow to implement this directive and the final arrangements, including the retrospective payment of appropriate benefits rates, were arrived at only after a case was taken against them in the European Court of Justice. As Ita Mangan suggests, "equality has a price and most Irish people affected by the Directive were not prepared to pay the price". Whether the Irish foot-dragging was excusable, given the economic and political background mentioned by Gerry Mangan (p. 56), or not, the fact remains that the basic problem was one of costs, costs to be borne entirely by the Irish Exchequer because of a decision "taken in Brussels".[3]

Greater Expectations It is probably also the case that EC membership has indirectly affected public attitudes and expectations in relation to the Welfare State, although this would be difficult to prove. For instance, in relation to the Community's initiatives on the harmonisation of social security, Gerry Mangan concludes that, it "is difficult to establish the extent to which these activities had a real influence on the evolution of policy at national level". (p. 92) Ita Mangan agrees that there "is little evidence that decisions [in Ireland] are taken in order to bring us further into line with standards in other EC countries".

Blackwell is inclined in the opposite direction. "It is likely," he says, "that EC entry has had an effect on Irish social security provision over and above the structural changes that have been instituted. The increases in real levels of benefit which have occurred since 1973 – admittedly, from low levels in relation to earnings in many instances – probably have been influenced to some degree by a desire for a convergence in living standards towards those of the Community as a whole". (1990, p. 373).

Whatever about these uncertainties, a case can be made that expectations in Ireland have increased in two ways: firstly, through the knowledge of better provisions in other member states obtained through

[3]The important decisions "taken in Brussels" are, of course, taken by the Council of Ministers, i.e. the sovereign governments, which make subsequent tardiness in implementation less justified.

travel and migration, whether for reasons of work or otherwise, and through the media; secondly, through the exchange of information by the EC within smaller programmes, "observatories" and discussion forums. Ita Mangan mentions these latter at the end of Chapter 5. One specific development exemplifies what is undoubtedly a more general process, although it does not, in fact, involve increased direct costs. In the second EC Programme to Combat Poverty, a project for the long-term unemployed in Dublin established contact with other projects for the long-term unemployed in other countries, and a group from Dublin exchanged visits with a group from a German project. The purpose of the exchange, within what was an experimental programme of local anti-poverty initiatives, was, in principle, to exchange knowledge and experience with a view to improved expertise and greater effectiveness. Members of the group from Dublin who were unemployed discovered that they could not receive unemployment assistance in respect of the period of their visit abroad, whereas unemployed persons from the German project had no such disadvantage. Afterwards submissions were made to the Irish authorities and the regulations were altered to cover travel abroad for a limited period by unemployed persons.

In summary then, membership of the EC has probably led to increased demands on the Irish Welfare State, and increased charges on the Irish Exchequer. If so, has this been matched by increased resources to meet those demands?

Increased Resources for the Welfare State

Membership of the EC could have led to increased resources for the welfare state in Ireland in three ways:

- by increased prosperity overall which, through fiscal buoyancy, could have meant more public funds for social purposes
- by improvement in labour force participation leading to less reliance on welfare and an expanded tax and contributions base
- by direct grants to the Irish Exchequer.

Once again, while the evidence is lacking or inconclusive, it is worth rehearsing the arguments in each case.

Increased Prosperity Has EC membership meant greater prosperity for Ireland? A good deal of attention has been devoted to this question in recent years (NESC, 1989; Foley and Mulreany, 1990; Keatinge, 1991; O'Donnell, 1993). Even among those who are strongly supportive of Ireland's participation in European integration, the answer is not clearly and unambiguously positive. NESC highlighted the fact that the gap between the standard of living in Ireland, as measured by GDP per head, and that in the better-off member states has not narrowed since 1973. In 1975, GDP per head in Ireland was 63% of the average for the EC12, as it was 14 years later in 1989 (1989, p. 117). Mulreany and Foley put it more starkly. "The broad summary of Ireland's position and performance in the European Community is quite bleak" (1990, p. 24). As for the explanations: "[t]he reasons why no convergence took place are complex and not fully understood" (Bradley, Fitzgerald and Kearney, 1992, p. 4).

In this volume, (Chapter 2) Larry Bond has summarised the evidence to date but has also emphasised the limitations of GDP-per-head as a measure of progress and a measure for comparison. The Irish economy has grown faster than the Community average but our population has grown too, and, therefore, we have not improved our position relative to our neighbours in Europe. If our overall standard of living has improved in absolute terms, it has not improved in relative terms, which was our ambition: we may be more prosperous overall but our problems have increased and it would be difficult to argue that our capacity to deal with them has improved.

Labour Force Participation While there may be no causal connection, the period since Ireland's accession to the EC has been one of prolonged failure as far as employment and unemployment are concerned. The fact that we have had a comparatively large agriculture sector, bound to decline, and increasing numbers of young people coming onto the labour market represented daunting challenges. Larry Bond has presented the full story in Chapter 2. In the early years of membership, employment growth rates in Ireland exceeded the average for the EC, but our performance disimproved subsequently. As already mentioned in this chapter, our level of unemployment is exceedingly high by historic standards and from a comparative point of view. Women's participation in the labour force is low and their participation rate has increased more slowly than in other European countries and even more slowly than in other newly industrialising countries. Within the labour force the gap is widening between the two categories in Gerry Mangan's classification, "people with a stable and well paid job" and "people with unstable employment characterised by low pay and low social security cover"(pp. 43, 104). Far from increasing its tax and contributions base, Ireland is having to cope with higher levels of dependency.

Direct Grants The EC provides, and has provided, direct grants to the Irish Exchequer through what are now known as the Structural Funds, the European Regional Development Fund (ERDF), the European Social Fund (ESF) and the Guidance Section of the European Agricultural Guidance and Guarantee Fund (EAGGF). The "Agricultural" Fund is directed at improving productivity in the agricultural sector and the ERDF is concerned with infrastructural development; only the ESF could be expected to have a direct impact on social policy. This is discussed by Ita Mangan in Chapter 5.

The ESF was conceived of as an economic measure, to promote activities, especially training, which would facilitate recruitment to the labour force. In practice, it is also used to support highly desirable activities with a negligible if any economic purpose such as compensatory education for the socially disadvantaged, training and support for persons with handicaps and even certain categories of third-level education. In some cases, these are additional activities over and above what the Irish authorities would otherwise fund. Even where there is not additionality, the availability of ESF monies – and monies from the other funds as well – has undoubtedly freed Irish funds for other social purposes. This led to improvements in social service expenditure in the 1970s, the advantages of which have lasted, but this effect could not be sustained or repeated.

The Balance Sheet As other authors have found, it is virtually impossible to balance the "costs" and "benefits" for Ireland of EC membership. Our purpose in this section was more limited and more tentative: to indicate the implications of EC membership, both positive (extra resources) and negative (additional needs), on the Irish Welfare State. Statements of cause and effect are too hazardous. However, our review of the preceding chapters has produced two dominant impressions: on the one hand, worsening social problems within a still comparatively underdeveloped economy; on the other hand, despite greater prosperity in absolute terms, no significant improvement in the availability of resources for dealing with the problems.

IRISH PROBLEMS: IRISH SOLUTIONS?

Even if it can be argued that the Irish Welfare State has not gained from the EC has it not still a creditable record, as we have shown in the first section of this chapter? Why look to the EC for assistance in this regard if we can deal with our own social problems ourselves? Unfortunately, despite a high level of expenditure on the welfare state, we are still not able to deal with our own social problems very well, and the kind of welfare state we have developed, and are continuing to develop, is creating its own problems. In the first instance we ourselves must acknowledge and analyse these problems and look for ways of dealing with them by strategic policy planning of our own.

One of the lessons of the NESC analysis of Ireland in the EC is that we assumed too easily that the solutions to our economic development problems, particularly in the agricultural sector, would come from Europe: we relied on EC policy-making and neglected policy-making for ourselves. The same mistake should not be made in relation to social policy. After analysing the situation we may find that the EC has an important role to play, but we need to know ourselves what we want to achieve.

We have two major challenges to confront. The first is to deal with the perverse social effects of the existing Irish Welfare State by reforming it; the second is to find a way of reconciling high and increasing levels of needs with the limits on the availability of resources.

We are alerted to the fact that existing policies have limited effectiveness, or even unintended adverse effects, when we contrast the high level of spending on the Welfare State, cited earlier in this chapter, with the persistence of extensive social problems. We subsumed these problems under the general heading of social exclusion and set them forth in Chapter 1 as a reminder of where we were starting from. It can be argued that social exclusion is not just the part of the body politic that social policy cannot reach, that it is not just evidence of the inevitable shortcomings of social policy, but that it is in a sense caused by the set of social policies, the model of Welfare State, we have adopted. The argument is put in two ways. The first is that we have a "pay related Welfare State" (O'Connell and Rottman, 1992) or what Tussing called, with reference to the United States, "a dual welfare system" (1975). A pay related Welfare State is one in which the better off you are the more you benefit from state policies. There is one set of provisions, the higher levels of education and the tax allowances for health insurance, private pensions and house purchase, which benefit the well-off and reinforce their security; there is another set of provisions, social welfare, public housing and education at the lower levels which are of benefit to the less well off but keep them in their relative insecurity. Breen and his colleagues, in their recent analysis of Irish society, indict the Irish Welfare State even more strongly. They argue:

(a) that the state plays an inordinate role in determining the structure of Irish society;

(b) that the results of state policies, and, in particular, patterns of public expenditure in the 1960s and 1970s, have been a reconstruction of the class structure which today allows for little social mobility and reproduces a marginalised underclass.

Such social exclusion as exists in Ireland is, then, according to this analysis, to an extraordinary extent due to the operation of state policies. The authors stress that "what is striking about the Irish case is the very direct nature of the link between public *expenditure* and the viability of class positions".

> The extent to which the State underpins the class structure can be gauged *via* some straightforward statistics. Of the population of three and a half million, roughly one and one quarter million are in full-time education or under school age. Of the remaining two and a quarter million, 1.3 million are in the labour force, of which around 1.05 million are at work. Of this latter figure, between a quarter and one third are employed in the broadly defined public sector. Just less than a further million people are not in the labour force nor in full-time education. The number of recipients of social welfare payments (including unemployment compensation, old age pension, disability benefits, and so on) is approximately three quarters of a million, with the total number of beneficiaries of such payments numbering 1.3 million. Figures such as these show the pervasiveness of the direct financing of Irish society by public expenditure. (pp. 219-220).

The state's shaping of society, these authors suggest, and the underpinning of the class structure, is effected through the three policy systems mentioned, those relating to education, the labour force and income maintenance. The analysis of Breen and his colleagues relates, of course, to the *effects* of State policies as distinct from the *intentions* of policymakers or the free *choices* of the electorate. In any case, their structures on the Irish welfare state have been countered by Callan and Nolan (1992):

> The Irish welfare effort is rather higher than might be expected on the basis of level of income per head...Detached comparisons with the UK, and more limited comparisons with other countries, suggest that this intervention is no less effective than in other countries. Thus, the greater degree of inequality in Irish incomes after government intervention can be traced back to greater inequality in market incomes.

There is little consolation in this. It means that the problems we have to deal with ("greater inequality in market incomes") are more daunting, and finding the right policies is more difficult.

If the kind of society we have, is to a considerable extent, shaped by the state then it can also be re-shaped by the state. Policy choices which were made in the past, and which produced adverse results, albeit unintended, can be and need to be re-examined. It can be argued that what we have done in the area of social policy over the past twenty years has been well intentioned, and has achieved the best possible results in very adverse economic circumstances. But it is remarkable how little discussion there has been on the causes and the consequences of major changes.

An example, which has been mentioned in this volume (pp. 69, 112, 113), is pensions policy. In the 1970s, it was proposed to have a national contributory pay related old age pension scheme which was seen to represent fair play and solidarity. This incipient policy has been now quietly put aside. We are rapidly developing a dual system or two-tiered system: a minority will continue to be financially cushioned in their old age with pay related private schemes in addition to the state contributory scheme; the majority will on retirement move to a basic flat-rate pension towards which they have made pay-related contributions during their working lives. As Gerry Mangan has argued, the funding and payment of contributory pensions is progressively redistributive and, given the ageing of the population, a pay-as-you-go national pension scheme may not be feasible. However, if the notion of social insurance is undermined and if the social services paid for out of taxation (whether called "contributions" or not) become services for the worst off, only then there may be social penalties. It is only by taking a comprehensive view that we get the right balance.

This debate about social policy decisions and solidarity could be quite academic. Nothing will change unless there is political awareness and a political will to change. There is some evidence that this awareness and will exists, in many if not all the political parties. The policy programme of the present Government expresses a commitment "to create greater equality throughout society". "We are firmly committed to eliminating inequality for all groups in society that have suffered from disability, disadvantage, or discrimination" (Fianna Fáil and Labour, 1993). It has been acknowledged that "Ireland is becoming a divided society". This must be confronted if "we want to shape a society which does not fail any of its people. We cannot and must not have a category of 'outsiders' who are convinced that their needs are not understood and their requirements are not catered for" (Fine Gael, 1988).

Even if the potential threats to Irish society are acknowledged, and the moral imperative to take remedial action is accepted at the political level, there is the further challenge of understanding that this remedial action cannot just consist of activities and programmes aimed at the excluded or disadvantaged themselves: more thorough-going reforms are required. What this means is a comprehensive strategic approach to social policy planning. The notion of integrating social planning with economic planning at the national level has been formally subscribed to for thirty years now but we have never got beyond an approach which consists of worthy but weak statements of social objective, a reiteration of the limits on social spending, and a catalogue of the incremental policy changes that had risen to the top of the political and administrative agenda at a particular time. The need for comprehensive social policy planning has been stated before (e.g. NESC, 1968); now when we are inclined to look to Europe to solve our problems we need more than ever to do the necessary groundwork within Ireland.

The reference to restraint on social spending brings us to the second major challenge. This arises because the Irish Welfare State, like that in many other countries, is caught between on the one hand, rising demands due to demographic and social change, unemployment and rising expectations and, on the other hand, pressure to restrict public expenditure. As the NESC put it:

> . . . social policies and the welfare state must continue to operate in a very constrained fiscal context. In the Council's view, structural reforms (by which is meant restructuring *within existing resources*) are necessary to enhance efficiency and ameliorate social inequalities. (1990, emphasis added).

Since the Treaty of European Union, public expenditure restrictions are regarded as even more compelling than before, because of the need to reduce the public debt in preparation for EMU.

The conclusion is unavoidable that the Irish Welfare State cannot respond to the increasing demands on it and at the same time not incur additional expenditure. If we cannot pay for necessary improvements from our own resources, then we have to resign ourselves to living in a society characterised by inequalities and divisions, and even the erosion of the Welfare State we have, or else we have to look elsewhere. If its social policy role is expanded, then our membership of the EC could offer an alleviation of our situation.

EC SOCIAL POLICY IN THE FUTURE

Against this background, what can we hope for from the EC? How is social policy in the Community likely to develop? O'Donnell, in his recent *tour d'horizon,* has complained, with reference to arguments about the need for an expanded Community budget and new budget mechanisms, that:

> . . . the discussion of this has been undermined by early introduction of possible political difficulties and exclusive focus on narrowly interpreted efficiency criteria. Those attitudes, which reduce discussion to cynical *realpolitik*, or an academic game, have never served the Community well, and contrast with the rigour and depth of the approach to the internal market programme. (O'Donnell, 1993, p. 65).

As an alternative, we can approach this issue of EC social policy in two stages by considering:

- first, what are the arguments in favour of an expanded role for the Community in relation to social policy?

– second, if the arguments are persuasive, to what extent are moves towards such an expanded role politically feasible?

The arguments in favour of an expanded social policy role can be summarised under five headings:

(i) *The instrumental argument:* EC member states are faced with common challenges in relation to the Welfare State at national level and should, therefore, develop collective strategies for dealing with them.

The "crisis of the Welfare State" has been under discussion for over twenty years. Some of the elements in that crisis, and the questions they pose, are rehearsed by Gerry Mangan in Chapters 3 and 7. Collins, writing on the lead-up to the Single European Act, 1987 highlights the role the Community could play in this regard:

> To move towards a new balance of public and family provision, taking into account Community, national, local and group responsibility for social need and a general acceptance of the broad guidelines of social redistribution seems very necessary . . . The Union will be required to play a part in seeking the new way forward if the member states are to hold together and to ease the social tensions they all face (Collins, 1986, pp. 102, 3).

(ii) *The compensation argument:* some member states at least, or perhaps all member states to some extent, have extra social costs to bear because of EC membership and therefore there should be a Community system of compensation.

Compensation here means two things. Firstly, there is the idea, notably articulated by Titmuss (1968), that one of the functions of social policy is at least partial compensation for "identified disservices caused by society . . . [including] international society". According to this way of thinking Ireland, for instance, should be compensated for costs incurred by the effects of EC policies. We have already raised this issue of social costs, among which unemployment must especially be considered:

> . . . unemployment compensation and labour market services have already borne costs as a result of the experience of integration . . .

> Further integration in the future may also create costs in the form of higher unemployment and the associated income maintenance and re-training burdens. At this point in the evolution of the Community, as a unified labour market emerges, there are grounds for communal sharing of the costs of unemployment compensation.
> (NESC, 1989, p. 515)

Secondly, while it is acknowledged that labour mobility within the Community must lead to the harmonisation of social policy provisions, NESC point out that the burdens of implementing harmonised policies may be very uneven as between member states, and that this is a further argument for cost sharing across the Community as a whole. Another aspect of labour mobility, in effect, migration, also calls for cost-sharing or compensation:

> . . . if migration from Ireland (or other peripheral regions with Ireland's unemployment/demographic profile) to other member states occurs on a significant scale, then the 'destination' states will benefit from the education, family support costs, etc., incurred by the 'origin' state in rearing and training the mobile worker.
>
> (*ibid.,* p. 511).

(iii) *The economic argument*: a European social policy is necessary to facilitate economic development in an integrated Community, and to avoid the adverse market effects of different levels of social provision in the different member states.

The "economic argument" consists of a number of arguments. First, many forms of social expenditure, especially, say, education, can be considered as social investment. If the EC is to become an efficient supra-economy, to rival the United States and Japan, then it must invest in its labour force. The EC education programmes already in existence represent some recognition of this principle, but it could also be more widely applied. Second, an efficient European economy requires mobility of labour and this has to be actively facilitated:

> In practice, there may be many social policy barriers to free movement and a social policy designed to assist economic integration and positively encourage labour mobility should, it can

be argued, tackle these. Are education qualifications transferable? Is health care as good? Is housing available? Are past pension contributions transferable and are new arrangements for social security satisfactory? Is child care available? Are there laws to prevent the racism and sexism in society which are, for many people, constraints on movement? Is environmental protection such that the air can be breathed and the water drunk? If the answer to any of these questions is 'No' then many people are not free to move.
(Kleinman and Piachaud, 1993, p.10).

To overcome these barriers to mobility, a much more extensive European social policy would seem to be necessary. This will have to go beyond the type of provisions in the Social Charter of 1989 which imposed obligations on member states regardless of their ability to meet them. Third, there is the "social dumping" argument referred to already in Chapter 1: the mobility of investment is likely to favour countries with lower factor costs, including the costs of social policies, and, therefore, some harmonisation of social policies at EC level is required.

(iv) *The equity argument:* within the European Community, proceeding towards "ever greater union", the continuation of gross inequalities between regions, between social groups or between individual families and citizens is intolerable and requires Community initiatives to remedy them.

(v) *The political argument:* the European Community cannot be sustained or developed unless there is, in some sense, a common identity and a commitment to it by its citizens in general, and this requires a framework of social policies at EC level.

These two arguments can be taken together. They are usually related to the notions of *cohesion* and/or *solidarity* but they are distinguished here according to the principles on which they are based: on the one hand, a principle of political philosophy or a moral principle; on the other hand, a principle of political necessity, or expediency.

As we saw in Chapter 1, economic and social cohesion has been a key objective to which the EC has subscribed for over twenty years. As between the original six member states there were no gross inequalities although there were less developed regions, such as the south of Italy. However, with the accession of Ireland in 1973, and of Greece, Spain and Portugal more recently, inequalities in the standard of living between member states, usually measured as GDP per head, and inter-regional inequalities, became highly visible. The peoples of the poorer countries and regions were promised greater prosperity from joining the Community: the message at the national level was reinforced by statements at the Community level. And so from one meeting of the European Council after another there issued an incantation of *cohesion* and *solidarity,* although, as we have seen exemplified by the Irish case, very little progress has been made towards achieving cohesion. The main instruments chosen, the Structural Funds, are too blunt and ineffectual in narrowing the prosperity gap between regions, and the whole subject of regional policy, and regional redistribution, is now being re-examined. The inequalities remain, still seen by many as a moral challenge within a grouping of nations that describes itself as a 'Community'. If these inequalities are to be reduced, the Community will have to exercise a more powerful redistributive function, going beyond the Structural Funds to a more extensive range of social policies.

O'Donnell (1993, p. 66) summarises the debate on this issue and outlines two possible approaches that have been proposed, either of which could be a feasible first step, far short of fiscal union, which could "be introduced at a low level, in recognition of the current political realities, and enhanced as the political cohesion of the Community develops". The first is "the development of a new instrument, operating through the social security system, to target aid to the most disadvantaged households in the Community" and the second "Community support for a minimum level of public good provision throughout the EC":

> Guaranteed provision of minimum levels of education, health, social security and public economic services will enhance the indigenous development potential of many weaker regions and member states.
>
> (Van Rompuy, *et al*, 1991 quoted in O'Donnell, 1993).

If cohesion is not tackled more seriously, it will not, then, be because of lack of ideas about how this could be done.

Increasingly, among those countries and interest groups and individuals for whom European integration is most important, the feeling of moral uneasiness has been added to, or replaced, by a feeling of political anxiety: European integration seems to be losing its attraction for many and this may be connected to the unfulfilled promises about cohesion and solidarity. A recent "Communication" from the EC Commission put it like this: "Maximum support for European integration will only be forthcoming if the 'social dimension' is developed". (Commission of the European Communities, 1992). The Padoa-Schioppa report put it more starkly: "imbalances in the distribution of benefits from Community policies may become so serious as to cause mounting political dissatisfaction with the Community in some countries, leading to non-co-operativeness and ultimately the threat of secession" (Padoa-Schioppa, 1986).

NESC in its 1989 analysis made the following connections: economic and monetary union will be impossible without a considerable level of political integration; greater political integration will be impossible without cohesion; cohesion cannot be achieved without a greater centralisation of taxes and expenditures in the Community, including significant social policy measures. Many have become convinced of the necessary connection between economic union and political solidarity, a connection highlighted by the dual ambition of the Treaty of Maastricht. The connection between political solidarity and social policy is just as close.

Coughlan, a critic of European integration, has rightly declared: "Solidarity is at the heart of social policy" (1992). He argues that the kind of group solidarity which exists within nation states makes social policy, involving redistribution, possible. Such a feeling does not, and cannot, he says, exist within a grouping such as the EC, and therefore, an EC social policy is impossible. This argument can be turned around: solidarity is impossible without social policy, or social policy is conducive to greater solidarity. One could accept Coughlan's first premise and still argue that within the European Community a sufficient degree of solidarity exists to make more extensive social policies practicable; following on from that, unless more extensive social policies are adopted, greater solidarity will not be achieved. In that sense it could be said that social policy is at the heart of solidarity.

Solidarity is connected with identity: national solidarity is related to a sense of national identity; if there is to be European solidarity there will have to be some sense of European identity, and European democracy. Lee has written recently (April 1993) about the aftermath of Maastricht:

> It may be that a real EC state will emerge as the distant end of an EMU tunnel. But what the Danish and French referenda have done is to expose the inadequacy of the functionalist approach to integration. The assumption that a political union would emerge from economic and monetary union has been undermined. Self-confident peoples – and many of the peoples of Western Europe, despite the levelling tendencies of the international media culture still have pride in their own identity – do not swallow the TINA argument, so beloved of the official mind: 'There is no alternative'.
>
> A real European union will ultimately be achieved, if ever, only through popular political participation, not on the basis of the percentage calculations of bureaucratic minds.

O'Donnell emphasises the importance of exploring the concept of European identity, which is, in turn, to be defined by particular values. He suggests that "in addressing a range of concrete problems and in acquiring the consent of the people that this be done at Community level, it will be necessary to draw on, and articulate, *values,* rather than rely solely on intergovernmental bargaining in secret" (1993, pp. 20,21). What are these values? He mentions democracy and liberalism and, more significantly, he cites the argument of French colleagues "that the social market economy, and the existence of the powerful welfare state is the real distinguishing feature of the European model" (*ibid.,* p. 21). If that is so, then developing a European identity upon which economic, monetary and political union can be built means conserving and integrating the national welfare states. He is pessimistic about the prospects in that regard because of the ideological, economic and demographic threats to the welfare state.

So, whatever about the arguments in favour of a European Welfare State, some version of it, how feasible is it as an objective?[4]

The Feasibility of a European Welfare State

While it is quite clear that Ireland could easily support moves towards

---

[4]The term *European Welfare State* has begun to be used in discussion. See, for example, the titles of the paper by Liebfried (1990) and the collection of papers edited by Room (1991).

a European Welfare State (Ó Cinnéide, 1993) there are strong countervailing forces. These forces are of three kinds. First of all there is the force of inertia and narrow economism. As we said in Chapter 1, for many policymakers, business leaders and politicians, the European Community is simply a Common Market, leading perhaps to an Economic and Monetary Union: the objectives of the exercise are economic objectives and the means to attain them are economic means. From this point of view, the fine words about cohesion and solidarity are justifiable rhetoric, but the arguments stated above are not acknowledged, much less dealt with.

Secondly, there is a reluctance to let additional powers, above the very minimum, pass from the national level to a transnational entity: "none of the member states appears eager any more to transfer large parts of sovereignty to the Community level" and "the political conditions for a strategy based on federalist ideas are not good (Teague, 1991). As we have seen (Chapter 1), the Treaty of Maastricht includes a provision about subsidiarity which for some member states represents the culmination of a campaign to restrict the growth of centralised Community power. The debate in a number of countries on the Ratification of Maastricht has focused on this very issue. This has been the case in Denmark, France and the United Kingdom; only in Denmark was there an anxiety that further European integration would lead to a *reduction* in Welfare State benefits.

Thirdly, there is in many countries a flowing tide of market liberalism which is expressedly inimical to the welfare state at the national level, and no more favourable to it at European level. Indeed, it has been argued that the European integration project sustains, and is sustained by, what could be called extreme right-wing economic thinking:

> . . . the internationalization of economic policy-making has meant a strengthening of the influence of conservative finance ministers and central bankers, a process in which wage-earners and unions have been the losers. The new 'consolidation doctrine' prevalent among policy-makers has meant a continuation of deflationary policies, an emphasis on private not public spending, and a redistribution of income towards profits, as supposedly the only route towards higher investment and hence more jobs in the long run. So far, the role of the EC has been as a facilitator of rather than a counterweight to this process: 'the EC Commission's policy

prescriptions tend to provide semi-technical justification for the dominant strategy' . . . Greater economic and monetary integration will lead not to the creation of the interventionist Keynesian Euro-state warned against by Mrs. Thatcher, but rather the institutionalization at the European level of the current liberal minimal state orthodoxy.

(Katseli 1989, quoted in Kleinman and Piachaud, 1993).

This apparent tendency towards market liberalism must be qualified in two ways. In the first place, its very existence could be said to demand "an equal and opposite reaction". As Kleinman and Piachaud conclude, "in the emerging European economic space workers will be weaker. There is therefore a political need to compensate them through the creation of a European social space". (1993, pp. 14,15). There is also a certain volatility in political thinking throughout Europe. The advantages of economic development based on economic integration are perceived, but so too are the prospects of social disaster linked to the politics of the extreme right. The attractions of unbridled market liberalism could suddenly pale. This may already be the case as instanced by the initiative of the Belgian government (May 1993) calling for a reassessment of the Maastricht Treaty criteria for the third stage of EMU on the grounds that they are too deflationary in an era of depression and high unemployment.

Consequently we are not inclined to conclude here on a negative note, with an unfavourable assessment of the prospects of a European Welfare State. Given our internal inequalities, and our relative under-development as compared with other member states, Ireland's interest lies in working towards more highly developed social policies at the Community level but equally we can argue that the very future of the Community depends on it. Whether using the term welfare state at the European level is helpful or not is something to be worked out. We are not on our own: we can take satisfaction from the existence of influences working in the same direction.

Positive Indicators

We have adverted to some of the negative factors which constrain or prevent the development of an EC social policy – the rise of neo-liberalism, the renewed emphasis on subsidiarity, the popular suspicion of, or disillusionment with, the whole EC project. These negative factors are articulated, or represented, by certain national governments, and through their influence by the Council of Ministers.

However, there are positive but less dramatic developments going on all the time regardless of these negative factors. As we have seen, the Treaty on European Union puts the role and functions of the EC in relation to education and public health on a firmer constitutional footing (p.8, Chapter 1). In both cases there is undoubtedly an impetus towards a more significant role for the Community. A recent EC conference on health services came to the following conclusions:

> There is now an opportune moment to promote better health in Europe and to strengthen public health. There is clearly a need for appropriate organisational structures to accomplish new tasks, particularly to assess the health impacts of other Community policies.
>
> . . . the increasing involvement of the Community in the health sector calls for a realignment and focusing of responsibilities in the Commission. While the Commissions role is complementary to that of Member States, this document identifies the need for a more strategic approach to health policy as well as specific requirements for co-ordinated action at European Community level.
> (EFILWC, 1991).

Even in the area of housing policy, where the EC has hardly any functions under the treaties and is precluded from action, there have been developments since 1989. The ministers responsible for housing in the member states have met every year in order to promote dialogue and exchanges of experience within the EC. At their meeting in Amsterdam in 1991 they said: "It is considered of importance to have continuous regard to the development of European economic, social and monetary policies and their influence on housing markets and policies, and assure a harmonious development between them". (Commission of the European Communities 1992, p. 114).

The inhibitions of some member states can be counterbalanced by certain positive indicators. These arise in two ways: from the involvement of important external interests at the EC level, and from an internal dynamic within Community institutions, the European Parliament and, more especially, the European Commission.

In the first place, there is the increasingly important role played by the social partners. As we have seen in Chapter 1, the Agreement on Social Policy attached to the Treaty on European Union envisages an enhanced role in policy-making for the social partners at EC level. As between employers' interests and workers' interests there are significant differences, but in the bargains to be struck about economic and social development it seems quite clear that there will be an expansion of social policy provisions at EC level.

The really powerful actors are the social partners' organisations. But European groupings of NGOs concerned with social issues are also having an influence that is not negligible. In relation to policy in respect of older people, *Eurolinkage*, which is a federation of national organisations concerned with the needs of older people, has played an influential role. The EC Commission has supported the establishment of the *European Anti-Poverty Network* (EAPN) which brings together representatives of national federations and representatives of European organisations concerned with aspects of poverty and exclusion. To the extent that such organisations can articulate progressive thinking in member states and make effective links with MEPs, and with national political institutions, they should be able to influence policy developments at EC level in a positive direction.

The European Parliament has also exercised, and will undoubtedly continue to exercise, its unique role in discussing and promoting social policy. In the lead-up to the adoption of the Social Charter in 1989, the Parliament adopted a radical approach to European social policy although the decision of the Council was in the event much more conservative. The increasing power of the Parliament *vis-a-vis* the Council bodes well for the future of social policy.

The role of the Commission in relation to social policy is also of great importance. The present President of the Commission, Jacques Delors, has always emphasised the connection between social development and economic development. The relevant services of the Commission have, in general, been forward looking as far as social policy is concerned.

The way the Community has raised and dealt with the issue of social exclusion provides a good example of the role of the Commission in an initiative at European level which from a modest beginning has come to have the potential for widespread and long-term action by the Community. The year 1989 was a good year for social policy in Europe. Three things happened which have been mentioned separately in Chapter 1 but are part of a pattern. The Social Charter was adopted which opened with an acknowledgement, *inter alia*, that "in order to ensure equal treatment, it is important to combat every form of discrimination . . . and . . . in a spirit of solidarity it is important to combat social exclusion". That year the second European programme to combat poverty was coming to an end and, in order to keep up the momentum of discussion and innovation, the third programme "to foster economic and social integration of the least privileged groups", now called *Poverty 3*, was launched to follow the second without a break. And lastly, the Council of Ministers, under the French Presidency, adopted a resolution on social exclusion (89/C277/01).

The resolution emphasised "that combating social exclusion may be regarded as an important part of the social dimension of the labour market", recognised that social exclusion results from structural changes in European societies and that to deal with it economic development, policies have "to be accompanied by integration policies of a specific, systematic and coherent nature". The resolution urged member states to deal with social exclusion through their own social services and called on the Commission to monitor and report on progress. The Commission did two things: it established an 'observatory' or network of correspondents, in effect, a system of annual national social reports; it also established an Inter-Service Group, representative of all the relevant Directorates General, "with a view to encouraging greater consideration for social exclusion in all Community policies". This group presented a comprehensive report on EC initiatives related to social exclusion to a conference in Brussels in April 1992.

The conference was addressed by the President of the Commission and attended by a broad cross-section of interested parties from all the member states, and from the European organisations representing the social partners and the non-governmental organisations. This was followed in turn by a "Communication from the Commission" entitled *Towards a Europe of Solidarity: Intensifying the Fight against Social Exclusion, Fostering Integration*, published just before Christmas [1992

COM (92)542 final]. The reason for issuing the document is set out at the beginning.

> At a time when perspectives are opening up for a gradual achievement of Economic and Monetary Union as well as Political Union, the Community cannot ignore situations which reflect, by their very existence and their scale, the need for a balanced construction of Europe, i.e. the need to combine economic ambitions with a concern for internal cohesion and its social dimension.

The Commission analyses the extent and nature of social exclusion, reviews the existing policies and activities of the Community which are relevant to a consideration of social exclusion and lays the groundwork for further action "which would be more vigorous than in the past but nevertheless taking into account the limitations in competence, resources and means". Overall, the Commission expresses a commitment:

> . . . to devising the policies and measures to be taken by the most appropriate players and to promoting a Europe of greater solidarity, while rejecting fatalistic acceptance of social exclusion and recognising that respect of human dignity is something to which all citizens have a right . . .

Of course, a document like this will be a dead letter unless the Council of Ministers, representing the member states, authorises the policy initiatives which will make a real difference. But it is evidence of an internal dynamic leading in a certain direction and an earnest of what the Community's role could be.

The next major step forward will be the publication of a Green Paper on Social Policy later in 1993 by the EC Commission, when and if the treaty on European Union has been ratified. This Green Paper will set out a policy agenda for the years ahead. Overall, it will take account of recent economic and social developments which have implications for social policy; it will mark the end of the period of the action programme on the implementation of the *Social Charter;* it will show how the new provisions on social policy in the Maastricht Treaty will be implemented. The preparation of the Green Paper provides an opportunity for suggestions and inputs by all relevant parties, including the member states. This is an opportunity which Ireland should not miss.

If Ireland is to have credibility in making recommendations about an EC Green Paper, it has to be able to convey a sense of purpose in relation to domestic social policies. The National Economic and Social Council in its comprehensive report, *A Strategy for the Nineties: Economic Stability and Structural Change* (NESC, 1990), laid the groundwork for an integrated approach to economic and social planning. The *Programme for Economic and Social Progress* (PESP) agreed between the government and the social partners in January 1991, and incorporating an *Agreement on Pay and Conditions,* followed through on the analysis, but only to a limited extent. The period of the Agreement and the Programme is coming to an end, and 1993 will see the next round of analysis and negotiation. NESC is preparing an updated strategic report. The National Economic and Social Forum is being established to provide the means for widespread consultation on policy issues. At the end of the year there may be a new programme to follow the PESP. This is a time when the relevant interests could clarify social policy objectives and adopt a plan which would give equal emphasis to economic and social issues, something long promised but never achieved.

A comprehensive planned approach to policy would enable the Irish government to establish the extent to which Irish needs and the people's legitimate expectations are in line, or out of line, with the country's resources. More importantly, the preliminary analysis to be done could include an estimation of how needs and expectations relate to EC developments and policies. In this volume there are already some indications of issues which Ireland could raise in its submissions for the Green Paper:

- on *externalities,* there is the issue of EC compensation to meet the exceptional costs for Ireland relating to unemployment support and education

- on *economic and social cohesion* there is the issue of the limitations of structural policies, the recognition of social inequality and the need to contemplate more redistributive policies

- on the *EMU* there is the issue of the future of the Community's budget and its role in relation to taxation and social programmes generally

– on *social exclusion* there is the issue of the need to review the Welfare State at national level and the supplementary and complementary role the Community should play.

All these issues need to be faced by the Community.

The first EC Social Action Programme was drafted by the first Irish Commissioner, Patrick Hillery, following the first meeting of what became the European Council, in Paris in 1972, in which the heads of state and heads of government "emphasised that they attached as much importance to vigorous action in the social field as to the achievement of the economic and monetary union". Twenty years later, another Irish Commissioner, Pádraig Flynn, is responsible for what could be a quantum leap forward in EC social policy. Ireland should make its mark on that policy.

LIST OF ABBREVIATIONS

AIDS	Acquired immune deficiency syndrome
CAP	Common Agricultural Policy
CEC	Commission of the European Communities
CEEP	European Centre of Public Enterprise
COMETT	Community Action Programme in Education and Training for Technology
CSO	Central Statistics Office
EAGGF	European Agricultural Guidance and Guarantee Fund
EAPN	European Anti-Poverty Network
EC	European Community
ECJ	European Court of Justice
EFILWC	European Foundation for the Improvement of Living and Working Conditions
EMU	Economic and Monetary Union
ERASMUS	European Action Programme for the Mobility of University Students
ERDF	European Regional Development Fund
ESF	European Social Fund
ESRI	Economic and Social Research Institute
ETUC	European Trade Union Congress

FÁS	Foras Aiseanna Saothair (Training and Employment Authority)
FEANTSA	Federation Europeene D'Associations Nationales Travaillant Avec Les Sans-Abri (The European Federation of National Associations Working with the Homeless)
IAPF	Irish Association of Pension Funds
ILO	International Labour Organisation
MEP	Member of the European Parliament
MISSOC	Mutual Information System on Social Protection
NESC	National Economic and Social Council
NGO	Non-Governmental Organisation
NOW	New Opportunities for Women
OECD	Organisation for Economic Cooperation and Development
PESP	Programme for Economic and Social Progress
PRSI	Pay Related Social Insurance
SEA	Single European Act
SEM	Single European Market
UNICE	Union of European Employers Organisations
VHI	Voluntary Health Insurance Board

BIBLIOGRAPHY

Atkinson, A. B. (1991) *Poverty, Statistics and Progress in Europe,* STRICERD Discussion Paper WSP/60, London: LSE.

Baldwin, R. (1989) *The Growth Effects of 1992,* Economic Policy Vol. 9.

Blackwell, J. (1990) *The EC Social Charter and the Labour Market in Ireland* in Foley, A. and Mulreany, M. (eds) *The Single European Market and the Irish Economy,* Dublin: IPA.

Boulding, K. E. (1967) *The Boundaries of Social Policy,* Social Work, Vol. 12, No. 1 pp. 3-11, quoted in Titmuss, R. M. (1967) *The Subject of Social Administration* in Commitment to Welfare (1968), London: George Allen and Unwin.

Breen, R., Hannan, D. F., Rottman, D. B. and Whelan, C. T. (1990) *Understanding Contemporary Ireland,* Dublin: Gill and Macmillan.

Bradley, J., Fitzgerald, J. and Kearney, I. (1992) The Role of the Structual Funds: Analysis of Consequences for Ireland in the Context of 1992 in Bradley, J. *et al.* (1992) *The Role of the Structural Funds,* Dublin: ESRI.

Bradley, J., Fitzgerald, J. and McCoy, D. (1991) *Medium Term Review, 1991-1996,* Dublin: ESRI.

Bulmer, George and Scott (eds. 1992) *The UK and EC Membership Evaluated,* London: Pinter Publishers.

Callan, T. *et al.* (1989) *Poverty, Income and Welfare in Ireland,* Dublin: ESRI.

Callan, T. and Nolan, B. (1992) Income Distribution and redistribution: Ireland in Comparative Perspective in Goldthorpe, J. H. and Whelan, C. T. (eds. 1992) *The Development of Industrial Society in Ireland* (Proceedings of the British Academy, 79), Oxford: Oxford University Press.

Cecchini, P. (1988) *The European Challenge 1992: The Benefits of a Single Market,* Aldershot: Wildwood House.

Central Statistics Office (1985) *Census of Population of Ireland 1981,* Volume III, *Household Composition and Family Units,* Dublin: The Stationery Office.

Central Statistics Office (1991) *Statistical Bulletin,* September 1991, Dublin: The Stationery Office.

Central Statistics Office (1992a) *Labour Force Survey 1991,* Dublin: The Stationery Office.

Central Statistics Office (1992b) *Live Register Statement 1992,* Dublin: The Stationery Office.

Chassard, Y. and Quintin, O. (1992) Social Protection in the European Community: Towards a Convergence of Policies, paper to the *International Conference on Social Security: 50 years after Beveridge,* University of York, England, 27-30 September 1992.

Collins, D. (1986), Policy for Society in Lodge, J. (ed. 1986) *European Union: The European Community in Search of a Future* New York: St. Martins Press.

Commission of the European Communities (1981) *Final Report from the Commission to the Council on the First Programme of Pilot Schemes and Studies to Combat Poverty,* COM (81) 769 final.

Commission of the European Communities (1988a) *Social Dimension of the Internal Market,* SEC (88) 1148, Brussels, 14 September 1988.

Commission of the European Communities (1988b) *Interim Report on a Specific Community Action Programme to Combat Poverty,* COM (88) 621 final (28 November 1988), COM (88) 826, in Social Europe, Supplement 2/89, CEC, Directorate General for Employment, Social Affairs and Education.

Commission of the European Communities (1988c) *Proposal for a Council Decision establishing a Medium-Term Community Action Programme to Foster the Economic and Social Integration of the Least Privileged Groups* (21 December 1988), COM (88) 826, in

Social Europe, Supplement 2/89, CEC, Directorate General for Employment, Social Affairs and Education.

Commission of the European Communities (1989a) Decision of 18 July 1989 establishing a medium-term Community action programme . . . 89/457/EEC, Official Journal of the European Communities, No. L224/10.

Commission of The European Communities (1990a) *Employment in Europe 1990,* Luxembourg: European Commission.

Commission of the European Communities (1990b) *European Economy No. 46,* Brussels: European Commission.

Commission of the European Communities (1990c) *Community Charter of the Fundamental Rights of Workers,* Luxembourg: Office of the Official Publications of the European Communities.

Commission of the European Communities (1991a) *Employment in Europe 1991,* Luxembourg: European Commission.

Commission of the European Communities (1991b) *European Economy No. 50,* Brussels: European Commission.

Commission of the European Communities (1991c) *European Economy Supplement A, No. 2/3,* Brussels: European Commission.

Commission of the European Communities (1991d) *European Economy Supplement A, No. 10,* Brussels: European Commission.

Commission of the European Communities (1991e) *Final Report on the Second European Poverty Programme* COM (91) 29 final, Brussels: European Commission.

Commission of the European Communities (1991f) *The Regions in the 1990s,* Luxembourg: European Commission.

Commission of the European Communities (1991g) *Communications on Supplementary Social Security Schemes in the Social Protection of Workers and their implications for freedom for movement,* SEC (91) 1332 final, 22 July 1991.

Commission of the European Communities (1991h) Commission

Report to the Council on the implication of Directive 75/129/EEC, SEC (91) 1639.

Commission of the European Communities (1992a) *Intensifying the Community's Efforts in the Field of Combating Social Exclusion, Working Paper prepared by the Interservice Group, Conference Combating Social Exclusion, Fostering Integration,* 2-3 April 1992, Brussels (Conference Paper).

Commission of the European Communities (1992b) *Towards a Europe of Solidarity: Housing, Social Europe, Supplement 3/92,* Luxembourg: Office for Official Publications of the European Commission.

Commission of the European Communities (1992c) Commission Report to the Council on progress with regard to the implementations of Directive 77/187/EEC, SEC (92) 857.

Commission of the European Communities (1992d) *Towards a Europe of Solidarity: Intensifying the Fight against Social Exclusion, Fostering Integration* (Communication from the Commission), COM (92) 542 final.

Commission on Health Funding (1989) *Report of the Commission on Health Funding,* Dublin: The Stationery Office.

Coughlan, A. (1984) Ireland's Welfare State in Time of Crisis, *Administration,* Vol. 32, No. 1.

Coughlan, A. (1992) The Limits of Solidarity: Social Policy, National and International, paper to International Conference, Social security 50 years after Beveridge, York, 27-30 September 1992.

Council of the European Communities (1972) *Communique (issued by the Nine after their summit conference in Paris, 12-20 October 1972)* in European Document Series (Dublin: Institute of European Affairs) No. 1, Spring 1993.

Council of the European Communities (1984) Decision of 19 December 1984 on establishing Community action to combat poverty, 85/8 EEC, Official Journal of the European Communities No. L2/24, 31.1.85.

Council of the European Communities (1989b) Resolution, of 29 September 1989 on combating social exclusion, 89/c 277/01, Official Journal of the European Communities, No. C277/1.

Council of the European Communities (1992) and Commission of the European Communities, *Treaty on European Union,* Luxembourg: Office for Official Publications of the European Communities.

Council of Europe (1991) *Recent Demographic Development in Europe.*

Courtney, D. (1992) Future Demographic Trends in the European Community, paper to Annual Conference of Retirement Planning Council of Ireland, 14 October 1992.

Curry, J. (2nd ed, 1993) *Irish Social Services* Dublin: Institute of Public Administration.

Cutler *et al.* (1989) *1992 The Struggle for Europe,* Oxford: Berg.

Deakin, S. and Wilkinson, F. (1989) *Labour Law, Social Security and Economic Equality,* London: Institute of Employment Rights.

Department of the Environment (1992) *Annual Housing Statistical Bulletin 1991,* Dublin: The Stationery Office.

Department of Health (1991) *Long-Stay Geriatric Statistics 1990,* unpublished.

Department of Labour (1991) *Economic Status of School Leavers 1990,* unpublished.

Department of Social Welfare (1992) *Statistical Information on Social Welfare Services,* Dublin: The Stationery Office.

Dunne, J., (1992) EC Social Policy After Maastricht, Address to *Conference of Institute of Personnel Management in Ireland,* 6 February 1992.

EFILWC, European Foundation for the Improvement of Living and Working Conditions (1991) *The Health Sector in the European Community 1992 and Beyond,* Shankill, Ireland: EFILWC.

Emerson, M. *et al. The Economics of 1992,* Oxford: Oxford University Press.

ETUC, UNICE and CEEP (1991) *Letter to the President of the Council of the European Communities, 31 October: Answer to Evaluation in Social Dialogue since 1989* Community Social Dialogue, Palais d'Egmont, 3 July 1992.

Faughnan, P. and O'Connor, S. (1980) *Major Issues in Planning Services for Mentally and Physically Handicapped Persons,* Dublin: NESC.

Fianna Fail and Labour (1993) *Programme for a Partnership Government 1993-1997,* Dublin: Fianna Fail and the Labour Party.

Fine Gael (1988) *The New Politics,* Dublin: Fine Gael.

Foley, A. and Mulreany, M. (1990) "Introduction" Foley, A. and Mulreany, M. (eds. 1990) *The Single European Market and the Irish Economy,* Dublin: Institute of Public Administration.

Golini, Cantalini and Lari (1990) *Technical Report on Demographic and Family Changes,* paper to seminar The Difficulty of Ageing: Current and Foreseeable Problems concerning Old Age Pension Schemes, Turin, 5-7 December 1990.

Grahl, J. and Teague (1990) *1992 – The Big Market,* London: Lawrence and Wishart.

Health and Safety Commission (1989) *Plan of Work for 1989-90 and Beyond,* London: HMSO.

Hughes, G. (1992) *Private Pensions in Ireland:* Ireland (OECD report: unpublished).

Industrial Policy Review Group (1992): *A Time for Change: Industrial Policy for the 1990s,* Dublin: Stationery Office.

International Labour Organisation, *The Cost of Social Security.*

Irish Association of Pension Funds (1991) *Investment Survey.*

Joint Committee on the Secondary Legislation of the EC (1984) Report on Proposals relating to Equality of Opportunity, Dublin: The Stationery Office.

Katseli, L. (1989) The Political Economy of Macroeconomic Policy in Europe, in Guerrier, P. and Padoan, P. C. (eds. 1989) *The Political Economy of European Integration,* Hemel Hampstead: Harvester, Wheatsbeef.

Keatinge, P. (ed. 1991) *Ireland and EC Membership Evaluated,* London: Pinter.

Keithley, J. (1991) Social Security in a Single European Market in Room, G. (ed. 1991).

Kennedy, K. (1992) Real Convergence, the European Community and Ireland, Presidential Address to the Statistical and Social Inquiry Society of Ireland, 14 May 1992.

Kleinman, M. and Piachaud D. (1993) European Social Policy: Conceptions and Choices, *Journal of European Social Policy,* Vol. 3. No. 1, pp. 1-19.

Laffan, B. (1985) *The ESF and its Operation in Ireland,* Dublin: Irish Council of the European Movement.

Lange, P. and Teague P. (1992) The Politics of the Social Dimension in A. M. Sbragia (ed) *Euro-Politics: Institutions and Politics in the "New" European Community,* Washington, DC: The Brookings Institution.

Lee, J. (1993) Europe: Where Now? *Irish Times,* 24 April, 1993.

Leibfried, S. (1990) Towards a European Welfare State, Americanization vs. Europeanization of Social Europe, unpublished paper to the Annual Conference of the Social Policy Association, Bath, 10 July 1990.

Lythe, C. (1991) Scotland and EC Regional Policy in the 1990s, in Day, G. and Rees, G. (eds.), *Regions, Nations and European Integration: Remaking the European Periphery,* Cardiff: University of Wales Press.

Marshall, T. H. (1949) Citizenship and Social Class in Marshall, T. H. (1963) *Sociology at the Crossroads,* London: Heinemann.

Moxon-Browne, E. (1991) The Legitimacy of the Union, in Keatinge, P. (ed. 1991), *Political Union,* Studies in European Union No. 1, Dublin: Institute of European Affairs.

McDowell, M. (1989) The Health Funding Commission Report: A Critical Commentary, Dublin: Centre for Economic Research.

National Economic and Social Council (1975) *An Approach to Social Policy,* Dublin: The Stationery Office.

National Economic and Social Council (1981) *Irish Social Policies: Priorities for Future Development,* Dublin: National Economic and Social Council.

National Economic and Social Council (1983) *Social Planning in Ireland: its Purposes and Organisational Requirements* (Report No. 68), Dublin: The Stationery Office.

National Economic and Social Council (1989) *Ireland in the European Community: Performance, Prospects and Strategy,* Dublin: National Economic and Social Council.

National Economic and Social Council (1991a) *Women's Participation in the Irish Labour Market,* Dublin: The Stationery Office.

National Economic and Social Council (1991b) *The Economic and Social Implications of Emigration,* Dublin: The National Economic and Social Council, Paper No. 90.

National Planning Board (1984) *Proposals for a Plan 1984-1987,* Dublin: The Stationery Office.

Ó Cinnéide, S. (1992) *Social Exclusion in Ireland, 1991-1992,* (part 1 of the Second Annual Report for the EC Observatory on National Policies to Combat Social Exclusion).

Ó Cinnéide, S. (1993) Ireland and the European Welfare State, *Policy and Politics,* Vol. 21, No. 2 April 1993.

O'Connell, P. J. and Rottman, B. (1992) The Irish Welfare State in Comparative Perspective, in Goldthorpe, J. H. and Whelan, C. T. (eds. 1992) *The Development of Industrial Society in Ireland,* (Proceedings of the British Academy, 79), Oxford: Oxford University Press.

O'Donnell, R. (1993) *Ireland and Europe: Challenges for a New Century* (Policy Research Series, Paper No. 17), Dublin: The Economic and Social Research Institue.

O'Higgins, M. and Jenkins, S. (1990) *Poverty in the EC: Estimates for 1975, 1980 and 1985* in Teekens and Van Praag (1990).

OECD (1989) *Education in OECD Countries 1986-87, A Conpendium of Statistical Information,* Paris: OECD.

OECD (1990, 1991) Economic Survey – Ireland.

Padoa-Schioppa, T. (1987) *Efficiency, Stability and Equality,* Oxford: Oxford University Press.

Programme for Economic and Social Progress (PESP), (1991) Dublin: The Stationery Office.

Pyle, J. L. (1990) *The State of Women in the Economy, Lessons from Sex Discrimination in the Republic of Ireland,* Albany: SUNY Press.

Rafferty, M. *New Wine in Old Bottles,* Poverty Today, Oct./Dec. 1992 Dublin: Combat Poverty Agency.

Rapid Reports Population and Social Conditions, various issues, Luxembourg: Statistical Office of the EC.

Review Group on the Treatment of Households in the Social Welfare Code (1991) Report, Dublin: Dept. of Social Welfare.

Ringen, S. (1987) *The Possibility of Politics,* Oxford: Clarendon Press.

Room, G. (ed. 1991) *Towards a European Welfare State?* Bristol: SAUS Publications (School for Advanced Urban Studies).

Room, G. (ed. 1993) *Anti-Poverty Action Research in Europe,* Bristol: School for Advanced Urban Studies.

Rottman, D. and Reidy, M. (1988) *Redistribution Through State Social Expenditure in the Republic of Ireland 1973-1980,* Paper No. 85, Dublin: The National Economic and Social Council.

Ryan, T. R. (1992) Health Care Insurance in Ireland, paper to seminar *Social Protection, a European Value: Challenge or Utopia* (organised by Institut de la Protection Sociale European), Dublin, 3-7 October 1992.

Sexton, J. (1988) *Long Term Unemployment,* Luxembourg: Eurostat.

Social Security Benefits, Northern Ireland and Republic of Ireland (1990) Belfast: Department of Health and Social Services, Dublin: Department of Social Welfare.

Staedlin, F. (1990) Social Policy, Social Charter, Basic Rights in *Social Europe* 1/90, Brussels: Commission of the European Communities, Directorate-General for Employment, Industrial Relations and Social Affairs.

Streeck, W. comment on Ronald Dore *Rigidities in the Labour Market,* Government in Opposition Vol. 23 No. 4 Autumn 1988.

Teague, P. (1991) Industrial Reconstruction or Market Completion? Irish Interests and the 1992 Programme – a review of the National Economic and Social Council Report on the European Community: Performance, Prospects and Strategy, *Administration,* Vol. 38 No. 4.

Teekens, R. and Van Praag, B. (1990) *Analysing Poverty in the European Community,* Luxembourg: Eurostat.

Teekens, R. and Zaidi, A. (1990) *Relative and Absolute Poverty in the European Community* in Teekens and Van Praag (1990).

Thompson, G. (1991) The Role of Economics of Scale in Justifying Free Trade: the Canada/US Free Trade Agreement and Europe 1992 Programme Compared, *International Review of Applied Economics,* 5.1.

Titmuss, R. M. (1968) Welfare State and Welfare Society in Titmuss, R. M. (1988), *Commitment to Welfare,* London: George Allen and Unwin.

Tussing, A. D. (1975) *Poverty in a Dual Economy,* New York: St. Martins Press.

Van Hove, N. and Saunders, G. (1990) The Single European Market: An Overview in Foley, A. and Mulreany, M. (eds.) *The Single European Market and the Irish Economy,* Dublin: Institute of Public Administration.

Rompuy, P. V., Abraham, F. and Heremans, D. (1991) Economic Federalism and the EMU in *The Economics of EMU, European Economy,* Special Edition.

Venturini, P. (1989) *1992: The European Social Dimension,* Luxembourg: Office for Official Publications of the European Communities.

Wedderburn, L. (1991) *Employment Rights in Britain and Europe,* London: Lawrence and Wishart.

AUTHORS' BIOGRAPHIES

Noreen Kearney qualified as a psychiatric social worker and worked in the Eastern Health Board before moving to TCD where she is a senior lecturer in social work. She has a long-standing interest in poverty and social deprivation and has been a member of successive government committees established since 1974 to research and develop new ways of dealing with poverty and its causes. She is currently vice-chairperson of the Combat Poverty Agency. She has served on various statutory and voluntary boards including the Eastern Health Board, the Council for Social Welfare of the Catholic Hierarchy and the Irish Association of Social Workers, of which she is a former president. She is at present head of the department of Social Studies in Trinity College, Dublin.

Larry Bond is a graduate of UCD in Politics and Philosophy, and is Head of Information in the Combat Poverty Agency. Previously he worked as a research officer in the Jesuit Centre for Faith and Justice, concentrating mainly on unemployment and related issues. He is currently undertaking research on the political determinants of unemployment and has published a number of articles on this topic in *Doctrine and Life* and *Administration.*

Gerry Mangan is the chief executive of the Pensions Board. After graduating from UCD in 1970 with a BA in History and Politics, he was a secondary teacher for six years. He then joined the Department of Social Welfare and worked mainly in the EC section, before being appointed principal officer in the Planning Unit in 1986. In that post he was responsible for policy on pensions and other long-term benefit schemes, and advising on EC Commission proposals on general social security matters. He is a member of the National Pensions Board, shortly due to publish its final report on the future development of the pensions system in Ireland, and of the National Council for the Elderly and the Observation Network on Supplementary Pensions Schemes.

Ita Mangan is Special Advisor to the Miniser of State at the Department of Social Welfare. For the past four years, she has been Legal Advisor to the European Commission Office in Ireland dealing with citizens' rights and social aspects of the EC. She has been the editor of the National Social Service Board publications – *Relate,* the monthly information journal; *Entitlements for Unemployed People; Entitlements for the Over 60s* and *Entitlements for Disabled People*. She is the co-author of *Social Welfare for Women* (Attic Press, 1989) and is the editor of the Carnegie Trust publication on Irish Perspectives on the Third Age. She has contributed background analysis for the Report of the Commission on Social Welfare and for *Poverty and Social Policy* (IPA) edited by Joyce and McCashin.

Séamus Ó Cinnéide is a senior lecturer in Social Studies at St. Patrick's College, Maynooth, where he directs the Masters in European Social Policy Analysis. He is a graduate of the National University of Ireland and was called to the Bar in 1980. Since his 1970 book, *A Law for the Poor,* he has written exensively on poverty, child care and juvenile justice, community development and social policy generally. He is a member of the central management group of the third EC poverty programme, Poverty 3, with responsibility for the evaluation of the programme, and of the EC Observatory on National Policies to Combat Social Exclusion.